THE
DARLINGS
OF VERMONT'S
NORTHEAST KINGDOM

THE
DARLINGS
OF VERMONT'S
NORTHEAST KINGDOM

HARRIET FLETCHER FISHER

Charleston  London

THE
History
PRESS

Published by The History Press
Charleston, SC 29403
www.historypress.net

Cover image: H.R.C. Watson, C.C. Stillman, A. Phillips, E. Darling, H. Wardner and J.B. Estes. This photo was taken at White River Junction, State Fair, September 1915.

Cover design by Marshall Hudson.

First published 2008

Manufactured in the United Kingdom

ISBN 978.1.59629.380.9

Library of Congress Cataloging-in-Publication Data

Fisher, Harriet F.
The Darlings of Vermont's Northeast Kingdom / Harriet Fletcher Fisher.
p. cm.
ISBN 978-1-59629-380-9
1. Darling family. 2. Burke (Vt. : Town)--Biography. 3. Northeast Kingdom (Vt.)--Biography. 4. Farmers--Vermont--Burke (Town)--Biography. 5. Businessmen--Vermont--Burke (Town)--Biography. 6. Northeast Kingdom (Vt.)--History. 7. Darling family--Homes and haunts. 8. Dwellings--Vermont--Burke (Town)--History. 9. Fifth Avenue Hotel (New York, N.Y.)--History. 10. New York (N.Y.)--Biography. I. Title.
F59.B89F57 2008
929'.20973--dc22
                                2008004621

Contents

Contents

Foreword

It is with great pleasure that I write this foreword to Harriet Fisher's book about the Darling family from Burke, Vermont. As a niece of Henry Darling II (1898–1986), Harriet contacted me as a source of any information about the Darlings. We spent many delightful hours combing through pictures and relating stories to each other about the subject matter. I was blessed to have Uncle Henry in my life and he continued to bless me by sharing his life and family with me. As a young child, I would follow Uncle Henry around the Mountain View Farm as he checked on each barn, the remaining Morgan horses and the farmhouse. By the early 1950s, Henry and his wife Kathleen (my mother's sister) lived in the village of Lyndonville, so it was a treat to accompany him once a week to his farm. As we toured the barns, he would tell me about the Jerseys and Morgans and show me all the ribbons that had been won by them. The barns were as they had been left, as if someone had just closed the doors. There were still remnants of hay and grain and, of course, all the beautiful sleighs, wagons, harnesses, saddles and bridles. For an eight-year-old horse-loving girl, this was pure heaven. When the inspection of the farm was completed, Uncle Henry would "talk business" with the caretaker and I would head to the horse barn to ride.

Eventually, it was decided that the farm would be sold and the contents auctioned off. Uncle Henry asked me if there was anything on the farm that I would like to have. My reply was, "The ribbons!" In the end, he did save a sleigh made by his grandfather, Henry Darling I, which was hand painted with a landscape scene by a man in West Burke and also a carriage that I have since found in many pictures of the Morgans. I treasure these items because they were important enough to Uncle Henry to save them for his young niece who could only think about the shiny colored ribbons.

Uncle Henry has remained an important man in my life even though he passed on in 1986. His stories, the pictures and the gentle influence he shared with me are everlasting. This book is important to me because it puts all of the information I had in my head in sequential order. The Darling legacy has finally, completely been recorded in one place to share with others. Harriet has made the family come alive with the humorous stories and actual pictures of their daily lives. As I was reading the description of Henry Darling I, I remarked how it also describes the Henry Darling I knew and loved. They were both gentlemen and gentle men with a keen memory of past experiences, a great sense of humor and love of family.

From A.B. Darling to Henry Darling II, a span of over 150 years, the Darling family touched the lives of many people. Even my own ancestors were involved with them. My mother's father raised the prodigy Morgan, Bob Morgan, who went on to sire many grand champions for the Mountain View Farm. My father's father, a watchmaker, installed and tended the huge clock on the horse barn. It is sad to know this legacy has ended, but Harriet has preserved it well. Thank you, Harriet, for making these memories come alive once more.

Jane Howe Cameron
St. Johnsbury, Vermont

Acknowledgements

There are many people to thank for the help I received in finding information and photos for this book. First of all, I thank Jane Howe Cameron for all her encouragement, verifications and loan of photos through her connection to the Darling family. Jane and I have a connection of our own through the Bradley family. Her great-grandmother, Rosaline Bradley, married Charles Howe, and Rosaline's sister, Mary Ann Bradley, married my grandfather, Joseph Alfred Fletcher.

Thanks to the Friends of Burklyn, now the Burklyn Arts Council, who sparked my interest in starting research on Elmer Darling and Burklyn Hall years ago.

To Dr. Clive Veri, former president of Lyndon State College who felt my research warranted a lecture at the Vail Clambake in 1987, thank you. He helped me with some research, particularly in the early ancestry of the Darlings.

Thanks to Allen Hodgdon for allowing me to glean what I needed from the paper that he wrote in 1970 at Lyndon State College to describe Burklyn Hall. Architectural descriptions were not part of my vocabulary.

My thanks to Burke Mountain Club and the East Burke Library for the use of their images, and for the opportunity to peruse the wonderful scrapbooks at the Clubhouse on the Fifth Avenue Hotel in New York City and the scrapbooks with clippings of the Mountain View Farm and Burklyn Hall properties. My thanks include librarian Charlotte Downes and George Hayes, custodian of the clubhouse and grounds.

There are other individuals to thank for use of photos, material and information—Dwight and Arlene Davis, Phyllis Burbank and Robert Michaud, to name a few. There may be others whom I have failed to mention. Whoever you are, please know that I am forever grateful for your help.

Though he died in 1986, the last of this Darling line, I am forever grateful to Henry Darling II for his kind and thoughtful sharing with me some of his memories and stories from the lives of his beloved family.

Introduction

In 1949, Senator George D. Aiken, former governor of Vermont, gave an address at a meeting of the Northeastern Vermont Development Association at the Darling Inn in Lyndonville. In this speech he referred to three counties—Caledonia, Essex and Orleans—as the Northeast Kingdom. He wrote in a letter to me in 1968, "When I named the Northeast Kingdom years ago, it seemed appropriate because this area obviously held a tremendous potential for development of a prosperous economy based on a wide use of healthy outdoor recreation."

Though it was not known as the Northeast Kingdom when the early Burke Darlings were here, this is where they lived and raised their families. Their contributions to this large area and beyond have made a difference in benefits still being enjoyed by so many in the Northeast Kingdom today.

It was my pleasure to work with a volunteer group calling themselves Friends of Burklyn and to become familiar with the grand house, Burklyn Hall, which was built by Elmer A. Darling in 1908. I began researching the life of the Darlings, Elmer in particular, to learn about him and what he did. It was a fascinating study and I even gave talks on the subject in the area. I was also able to obtain pictures that helped link the past with what I saw at Burklyn.

In 1987, Lyndon State College president Dr. Clive Veri asked me to give the lecture at the annual T.N. Vail Clambake, an event that raised funds for scholarships and in honor of Vail himself, who used to give parties such as a clambake at his mansion, and who also was a great benefactor of the area. LSC is located on the former Theodore N. Vail Speedwell Estates on the hill above Lyndon Center. The title of my talk was "The Darlings and Their Contributions to the Northeast Kingdom"; I did not know then it would someday be the nucleus of a book.

Much has been written about the Darlings in newspapers, journals and reminiscences. It is my intention to put together in one place the lives and work of this family. I hope readers will be able to capture a glimpse into the lives and minds of these people and learn that what they did still has an effect on the lives of many people today.

In Sight of Burke Mountain

The house still stands on the hills in northeastern Vermont. Some have called it a mansion, others have called it a manor, but to Elmer A. Darling it was simply Burklyn Hall. The house, begun in 1904 and completed in 1908, sits squarely on the line where the towns of Burke and Lyndon meet on a ridge not far from Burke Mountain.

The house has a different owner and occupancy now, but Burklyn Hall may be considered the symbol of a man whose name lives on. Not only are Elmer Darling and his family remembered in these two towns, but also in distant places where their contributions to what is now known as the Northeast Kingdom, and beyond, continue to benefit many communities. This results as well in benefits to individuals in the communities.

The ridge, once called Bemis Hill and now known as Darling Hill, rises between the east and west branches of the Passumpsic River. Feeder brooks trickling and seeping southward down the wooded mountainside give rise in Newark to the Passumpsic. It meanders leisurely across flat meadows in East Newark and is joined by brooks, including Mill Brook, which comes tumbling off East Mountain and trips head over heels into the Passumpsic River on Route 114.

The West Branch of the Passumpsic begins in Westmore on the southern slope of Mount Pisgah at Lake Willoughby, and coming through Burke meets the East Branch north of Lyndonville near Folsom's Crossing. Fed by numerous streams all the way to Barnet, about thirty-four miles in all, the river ends as the Passumpsic and the waters flow into the Connecticut River at Round Island just below Fifteen Miles Falls.

Thus, Burklyn Hall is situated on land that slopes toward the valley of the Passumpsic, on the west side, and stands above the Passumpsic that runs along the road to East Burke on the east side. Burke Mountain is partly in Burke and partly in Kirby. The town line is very near the summit. The mountain rises nearly three thousand feet above the Passumpsic River. Generations of Darlings have been raised in the shadow of Burke Mountain, so it too may be considered a symbol of the Darling family for what it meant to them.

The house—Burklyn Hall.

Elmer Alfred Darling was born April 22, 1848, on a farm at the foot of Burke Mountain. Arthur F. Stone wrote in *The Vermont of Today*,

Outstanding among well-known figures of Vermont, Elmer A. Darling, whose career has been of singular variety, and interest, who now [1928] resides in a palatial residence called Burklyn Hall near East Burke, pays taxes in eight towns, is a moving spirit in all projects directed toward the advancement of several communities, and who belongs to one of the oldest families in the United States.

The Eight Generations of Darling American Ancestry

The first Darling ancestor in America was John Darling, a sea captain who emigrated from Darlington in the north of England in 1640. The name Darlington would crop up again a few generations later when one descendant ascribed the name to his farm in New Jersey. John settled in Kingston, New Hampshire. He and his wife, Mary Bishop, had five children, three sons and two daughters. One son named John was born December 21, 1683, in Salem or Andover, Massachusetts.

John, second generation Darling, married Mary Page and they had nine children: Abigail, Daniel, Judith, John, Naomi, Omesiphodous, Philip, Mary and Ruth.

The third-generation John, son of John and Mary Page Darling, was born in 1716 in Salisbury, Massachusetts. He married Hannah Morse in 1739. Of their nine children, one was a son named Peter, born in 1752 in Kingston, New Hampshire.

Peter of the fourth generation married Rebecca Burbank and they had nine children, one being a son named Ebenezer, born July 20, 1787, in Kingston, New Hampshire.

It was this fifth generation, Major Ebenezer, who established the generations of Darlings in Burke. He had served in the War of 1812 and came to Burke soon afterward. He married Abigail Fisher, who was born January 7, 1790, the daughter of Timothy Fisher of Claremont, New Hampshire, whose son, Timothy Fisher Jr., was one of Burke's prominent men. Ebenezer and Abigail had eight children, all born in Burke. They were Henry George, Charles Burbank, Alfred Burbank, Caroline M., Lucius Fisher, Abigail, Pamela M. and Scott E.

It is sad to relate that three of their eight children, Caroline M., Pamela M. and Scott E., lived short lives; all died at home of consumption, Caroline, born June 7, 1823, died July 17, 1842, age nineteen; Pamela, born March 9, 1831 (spelled Pamelia on the tombstone in Burke Hollow Cemetery), died June 11, 1856, age twenty-five; and Scott, the youngest, born July 1, 1833, died February 15, 1851, age eighteen.

A tintype, probably of Lucius A. Darling.

Lucius Fisher Darling, born August 4, 1825, also died at a young age. He was with his brother at the Battle House, the hotel Alfred Darling was managing for Paran Stevens in Mobile, Alabama. Lucius F. died there of yellow fever September 20, 1853, at the age of twenty-eight.

Ebenezer's sixth child, Abigail, listed as Abbie Darling in Child's Gazetteer, became the second wife of John W. Evans of Lyndonville. His first wife was Emily Fisher of Burke. No doubt Abbie Darling and Emily Fisher were related. That often happened in those days; a visiting relative might meet a future wife or husband. John Evans's third wife was Mary Colburn. John Evans "had born to him" four children: Emma F., Albert T., Caroline L. and Ella P. Ella was Abigail's daughter of this marriage and she died at age fourteen. Abigail died before her daughter.

Ebenezer's oldest son, Henry George Darling, seventh generation, born August 15, 1816, married Mehitable Whitcomb of Lyndon on June 15, 1845. Their children were Elmer Albert, Scott E., Louise and Lucius.

Lucius A. Darling, son of Henry G., was born June 1, 1857. He was the seventh generation of this line. He married Margaret McDonald. Their children were Pearl Enid and Henry George. Pearl was born August 3, 1892, but sadly, she died at the age of eight with "that dreaded disease, diphtheria" on March 3, 1901. The obituary says, "Little Pearl was a very bright, loving child, and her death cast a gloom over the entire village."

Henry George Darling II, seventh generation, was born August 13, 1898. In 1941, he married Kathleen Chaffee of St. Johnsbury Center. They had no children.

Ebenezer Darling

It is not known today how Ebenezer Darling happened to settle in Burke. By the time he arrived soon after 1812, much of the highland had been taken up along the central ridge. Burke Green in the center of town was already settled, so Ebenezer cleared land north of the Green with a view of Burke Mountain across the valley. On the other side of the valley against the rising hills was a district that became known as Pinkham. He could see the farm of a friend, Captain Timothy Fisher, and perhaps that is how he got his eye on Abigail Fisher, the captain's sister, who may have been visiting there.

It was probably well that Ebenezer did not start a farm nearer Burke Green, the first "village" in town, because it was a windswept location with drifted roads and steep hills. There was a town house, built in 1802, a public green and a burying ground, but it became abandoned as people left for better locations in Burke or elsewhere. By 1821, the town house was taken down and in a few years all the houses were gone. All that was left was the burying ground.

It was definitely a place with fierce and blustering winds. In the hurricane of September 1938, most of the beautiful tall pine trees in and around the little cemetery were blown down and caused much damage to many of the tombstones. But they were repaired and today it is a lovely, well-kept spot where one can find many familiar Burke names on the tombstones, proving that not all the settlers moved away; many of them apparently just moved elsewhere in the town.

The land Ebenezer cleared lay between the farms of Elder Hicks and Abner Coe. It was a hard struggle with the land just newly cleared to make a living for his large family, but it is just this kind of a life that develops talents and ability of the children. Those who lived long enough to develop careers proved it. Ebenezer took an active interest in town affairs, church and schools. In 1825, Ebenezer represented the town of Burke in the legislature.

The Burke Hollow Meetinghouse

This is the story of the meetinghouse where many of the Darlings of the early years attended services. The settlers of Burke wanted religious services and asked Elder Peleg Hicks to come to preach the gospel. Most of the people in town were Baptists and in April 1801 formed a society, which constituted the first religious group in town. They elected Elder Hicks as their pastor. It seemed that not all Burke people were Baptists, as disagreements arose and other denominations formed their own societies. The Congregationalists formed in 1807 and the Universalists in 1815. The various groups met in homes, then in the town hall located on Burke Green.

The people might not have agreed on religious beliefs, but they did agree to build a common meetinghouse. On April 2, 1825, people interested in building one drew up a constitution for the proposed meetinghouse. These pioneers met at the schoolhouse to bid for choice pews to raise the funds for building. They felt justified in spending the money, though it was hard to come by, for something so dear to New Englanders—a house of worship. Bids went as high as $40 and as low as $17, and the total raised was $1,714.75. Timothy Fisher Jr. got slip number seven and his brother-in-law, Ebenezer Darling, got slip number fifteen. The town pledged $150 to use the building for public purposes.

The building was to be forty by fifty-five feet. Ira Armington of St. Johnsbury was given the contract and Seth Clark of Burke was the master carpenter. Elder Palmer officiated at the "raising" with a prayer. This was the census at the time of the building: Baptists, fifty-seven; Congregationalists, fifty-three; Universalists, forty-eight; Methodists, some.

The building was dedicated in 1826, and services were to start the third Sunday of September. Lots were drawn for the dedication, and the Baptists got the services, with Elder Cheney of Derby preaching the dedication service. Lots were drawn to decide the order of services—Congregationalists the first Sunday of each month, Universalists the second, Baptists the third and the Methodists the fourth. There is no mention of who had the service in a month when five Sundays appeared on the calendar.

The Burke Hollow Meetinghouse.

Regardless of which denomination held the service, people came anyway. Only the preacher was changed. The famous Burke Singers, often fifty in number and probably a combination of all denominations, were renowned throughout the county. They raised their voices exuberantly from the balcony at the back of the house. "There were Squire Hall's thirteen children, all good singers, William Godding who could 'bugle' [yodel] so the call could be heard two miles away, all the Smiths—Sophia Wealthy, Frinda, Almon, and Charles; Capt. Lem Hall, fat, jolly and not always sober; the Fylers, the Trulls, and many others."

Electra Trull was the acknowledged chief of the singers. Her supremacy was disputed one time when a new family took their place in the gallery and remarked, "Mrs. Trull, you have been head here a good while. It's time others was head now." Whereupon Mrs. Trull marched across the gallery with her singing book. "If that's the case, we'll start a head at the other end." This story is told in the booklet that was printed during the one hundredth anniversary of the building of the church.

The meetinghouse's exterior is simple and symmetrical. Large paneled doors lead into the entry, where the old up and down saw that was used in the construction of the meetinghouse is displayed behind glass. The lumber was sawed out in the Burt Dolph mill on the Victory road.

Sixty solid box pews with latched doors seated about three hundred people, but often the aisles were filled with more than that in the old days.

Above: Interior of the meetinghouse. Note the solid box pews, the barrel pulpit and the balcony where the singers held forth.

Left: A reunion at the Burke Hollow Church, August 30, 1946. Henry is the last one at right; his mother, Margaret Darling, is in front, and next to Henry is his wife Kathleen.

The barrel pulpit, reached by a stairway and another latched door, is an example of the workmanship there. The old oil lamp chandelier still hangs from the ceiling. Identical box stoves were installed in 1828, and the building was painted in 1842. The belfry was installed in 1859.

The Baptists withdrew in 1855 and built a church in East Burke. The Universalists died out and the Methodists withdrew in 1858, also having built a church in East Burke. There is a Universalist church in West Burke; part of it is used for the village library.

As the societies became larger and built their own churches in town, the meetinghouse in Burke Hollow was no longer used. However, it was repaired through the generosity of Alfred B. Darling and rededicated to the service of God on June 28, 1896. In addition to the annual Old Home Day, which is marked with service in this beautiful old meetinghouse, it is occasionally opened for funerals, weddings or other special occasions.

Henry George Darling

Henry George Darling, Ebenezer's oldest son, was born August 15, 1816. He obtained a sound common school education and taught several terms in Burke schools. Henry still lived on his father's farm, helping with the large family, but he began to think about a place of his own. When he was about twenty-four, he went across the valley and started clearing the forest at the foot of Burke Mountain. "Almost single-handedly," as folks liked to mention, he created a farm of his own. Years later this became the McHarg place; now it is owned by Burke Mountain Academy.

On June 15, 1845, Henry married Mehitable Whitcomb, born October 22, 1820 (spelled Mahitable on the tombstone in Burke Hollow). She was the daughter of Cummings and Louise (Quimby) Whitcomb. Their children—Elmer A., April 22, 1848, and Scott E., December 21, 1851—were born on this farm.

"Just as most pioneers had to do of necessity," wrote Mabel Hall Walter in 1896, "Henry had acquired many skills from his father and neighbors so that he became an outstanding carpenter and craftsman. During the long winter months he built and sold sleighs and wagons, and was well respected for his workmanship."

In 1854, he moved his family to a farm in Sutton. Two more children were born here, Louise A., October 30, 1854, and Lucius A., June 1, 1857. By 1866, Henry found his health was failing with the severe climate and he moved his family back to Burke. Henry's brother, Alfred of New York City, bought a neat white house for them in East Burke village. Later it became the Bowman house.

Henry was a great conversationalist with a keen memory for dates and places. People gathered around Henry to hear him tell about the old times. He was highly respected for his keen sense of right and wrong, his gentleness and his refinement of character. He never complained during the years of his illness. He was a true philosopher. He had been a church member ever since his boyhood and his faith remained unshaken. Politically, he believed in the principles of the Republican Party.

Henry's youngest son, Scott E., born December 20, 1851, attended Kimball Union Academy in Meredith, New Hampshire, and graduated from Dartmouth College in 1876. He taught school for a couple of years, but because of failing health went to Colorado, where he worked on a cattle ranch. It seemed his health was much improved, but later in Texas he contracted malarial fever, which left him with weak lungs. He came home but, not improving, he went to the Adirondacks, hoping to regain his health.

The *Republican*, a weekly newspaper in St. Johnsbury, gives this account of Scott from November 21, 1885:

> *News has just been received of the death of Scott E. Darling. The* New York Tribune *of Tuesday says: "The friends of Scott E. Darling, nephew of A.B. Darling of the Fifth Avenue Hotel, were pained yesterday by the announcement of his death in the Adirondacks at the age of thirty-four. He was a companionable young man, remarkable for his great aptitude in acquiring information and his wonderful memory. He was born in Burke, Vt. where his body will be taken for burial. He was educated at Dartmouth college where he was graduated in 1876. On account of his health he went to Colorado where he engaged in cattle raising which he followed later in Texas. He contracted malaria and was obliged to take a sea voyage to the Bermudas. He has been in the Adirondacks since a year ago last July, making a brave but unavailing battle for life. He was unmarried."*

Henry didn't live long enough to see his son Elmer build Burklyn Hall, but the family had moved from East Burke village after Elmer bought and renovated Mountain View Farm, and he did live to see the farms become the showplace of the whole area. Henry must have enjoyed the handsome Morgan horses and the herd of registered Jersey cows. These cows produced the milk and cream for the butter and cheese made in the creamery behind the main house, products that went to the railroad every day to be shipped to the Fifth Avenue Hotel.

Henry died September 5, 1902, at age eighty-six. He was buried in Woodmont Cemetery in East Burke in the shadow of his beloved Burke Mountain. Mehitable died May 16, 1906.

Major Benjamin Whitcomb

Henry's wife, Mehitable, daughter of Cummings and Louise (Quimby) Whitcomb of Lyndon, came from "brave old stock," wrote Charles T. Walter in the *St. Johnsbury Republican*, Burke Centennial issue. Mehitable's great-uncle, Major Benjamin Whitcomb, was a pioneer hunter and trapper, and was "prominent in the early history of Essex County." He often spent months at a time in the wilderness, falling in often with Indians, camping and hunting with them. Naturally, the exploits of their ancestor were part of the Darling heritage and family stories.

One time in early winter, Benjamin Whitcomb found an Indian, alone and nearly starved. His gunlock having broken, he was unable to shoot game. Whitcomb fed and kept him for three weeks, trapped with him, divided the furs and gave him enough food to last him until he could get home.

Whitcomb served under General Putnam in the old French war, was in several fights and was then taken prisoner and carried to Quebec. He wrestled, ran and shot at marks with the Indians, but let them beat him so as not to offend them. After Colonel Ethan Allen took Ticonderoga, Major Whitcomb served as a scout.

General George Washington offered a major's commission to men who would go into Canada and shoot a prominent British officer in retaliation for the terrible massacres of women and children committed by the Indians who sided with the British. Whitcomb and two others volunteered, but one deserted. Whitcomb and his companion made their way toward Three Rivers and discovered that British soldiers and Indians were to move toward the line soon. The companion became scared, deserted and went to the enemy, telling them of Whitcomb's plans.

Whitcomb, undaunted, moved near to the camp to find a new place for his ambush. He did not intend to lose his major's commission. As the British column with Indian scouts passed by, Whitcomb watched for an officer whose rank appeared high enough to fill the requirement of Washington's circular. He finally saw an officer with a red sash around his waist and a long, white plume in his hat, riding on a splendid white horse. Major Whitcomb fired, saw the officer fall back and quickly hid himself. The Indians near the road saw the smoke of the gun and took off after him. The man he had shot was General Gordon, who died in half an hour, and the British didn't intend to let Whitcomb get away with it.

He managed to baffle and elude them, traveling all day and all night. All he had with him at the time he shot the man was some parched corn, which was all the sustenance he had for four days. He didn't dare to kindle a fire or shoot game because he knew that would give away his whereabouts. The fifth day he crossed the line into Vermont, but did not dare to stop at a house for food, fearing the inhabitants might be Tories. He shot an ox in a pasture, quickly cut out some steak and some skin for a pair of moccasins and ran into a deep swamp, where he dared to start a fire, roast some meat and eat it on the run. He finally reached Royalton and apparently stopped at a house to ask for food and rest.

The British had offered a thousand crowns for his head, and two thousand crowns for him to be delivered alive at any British post. After a time he joined a small frontier guard at Lancaster, New Hampshire, in a blockhouse where he felt secure, so on occasion he went out hunting. One day while he was out, five Indians grabbed him and hurried him off to Canada. They were about twenty miles from a British post where the Indians intended to give him up for the reward. They camped on an island in the St. Francis River, where they bound Whitcomb's hands and feet and tied him to two Indians, one sleeping on each side. Escape? Impossible!

Whitcomb recognized one of the Indians he had befriended years before and tried to gesture to make the Indian recognize him. About two o'clock in the morning he was wakened by gentle taps on his mouth to indicate silence. The bonds were carefully cut and a hand motioned to rise and follow cautiously to the river. The Indian handed him his gun, powder horn, ball pouch, knife and a bag of parched corn and said, "I now pay you—go, go." Whitcomb slipped into a canoe and pushed out into the river. The Indian gestured a farewell and turned back to camp. Whitcomb pushed back to shore and cut a hole in the other canoes, crossed to shore, cut a hole in his canoe, pushed it off and ran for his life. He pushed on day and night until he reached Massachusetts, the home of his early childhood, and there he stayed during the rest of the war.

He received his major's commission for his brave service to the cause of the colonies, and in his old age received a major's pension.

Charles Burbank Darling

Charles B. Darling, Ebenezer's second son, born in Burke June 24, 1818, attended Lyndon Academy and studied medicine with Dr. Brown and Dr. Sanborn. After graduation from the Allopathic College of Medicine at Woodstock in 1844 and from the Pennsylvania College of Homeopathy in 1852, he had a successful practice in Lyndon, Vermont. In *Successful Vermonters*, author William H. Jeffrey writes, "He was always pleasant, social, and genial, a real 'old school,' 'family physician,' one that it is always a pleasure to remember."

On December 9, 1852, Dr. Darling married Susan, daughter of Hiram and Caroline (Bigelow) Melvin. They had two children, Charles Melvin and Jennie L.

In those days doctors had students in their offices. Charles M. Darling III from New York City sent me this story about his grandfather in 1985.

> *There were several students in Dr. Darling's office and occasionally after a hard day's work, they planned some particular amusement for the night. Sometimes the program arranged called for a midnight raid on the neighborhood hen roost and inviting to the office some of the village boys for a feast at a time when the doctor was supposed to be in bed. But he was irregular about his hours and on more than one occasion unexpectedly came in and caught the boys in the act. His reprimand in such occasions was usually completed in the following gentle reminder, "Bad boys, bad boys!—don't you ever let me catch you stealing any more poultry. Give me a drumstick!"*

Dr. Charles B. Darling died June 19, 1861. His wife Susan Darling died in September 1861. The children were brought up by Mrs. Darling's relatives. Jennie L. married Colonel H.E. Folsom, division superintendent of the Boston & Maine Railroad. When William and Emma Fletcher moved to California in 1885, they sold their house to Mr. and Mrs. H.E. and Jennie (Darling) Folsom. The Folsoms moved the house my Great-Uncle William had built to another location on the street and built themselves a Dutch Colonial house on the site.

Dr. Charles B. Darling.

Charles Melvin Darling

Charles Melvin Darling wasn't even five years old when his parents, Dr. Charles B. and Mrs. Darling, died. He lived with his maternal grandmother, Mrs. Thomas Carter, at East Lyndon. He went to school at East Lyndon, but to the Methodist church at Lyndon Corner. When he was ten he went to live with his aunt and her husband, Mr. and Mrs. Charles Rogers in South Wheelock, and finished elementary school in the Old Red Schoolhouse.

Later Mr. Rogers bought a farm near Wheelock village, where Charles lived until he was twenty-one. He attended Lyndon Institute for three years, boarding in Lyndon Center at the home of Jeremy Pearl. He attended the Auburndale School in New Jersey that his uncle Alfred Darling had established. He had two years in the scientific course at Dartmouth College.

Alfred B. Darling of New York City advanced his nephews Charles—Charles B.'s son—and Scott—Henry G.'s son—some money in about 1880 to go into business for themselves. They bought a trail herd of about 1,500 Texas cattle at Ogallala, Nebraska, and put them on a range near Greeley, Colorado, where they had one hundred miles of range for grazing. It was a hard, cold winter and about half the herd died. They sold the remainder. In 1883 they bought some horses and cattle. For a while, Charles and Scott bought and sold stock. Their next move was to Texas, where they bought 640 acres on the Brazos River, increasing their land until they could graze about 1,500 cattle on the range.

During the winter, Scott had an attack of chills and fever, malaria. He went back east to recoup in the Adirondacks. He died there and Charles remained on the ranch until he could sell the cattle. He went back to the Clopper ranch in Colorado, where he had a large herd of horses. He purchased the Living Waters Ranch in Bennett, Colorado. There he was breeding and selling horses and enlarging his ranch to about three thousand acres. He fixed up an old log house, once a station for stagecoaches, which he made into a comfortable home.

In 1893, Charles sold out, as times were hard in Colorado, and came back east, where he went to work on his uncle Alfred's farm in New Jersey. He traced the pedigrees of valuable horses and Jersey cattle on Alfred's Valley Farm. He made up a catalogue for the horses and one for the cattle. It had been painstaking work and required much research in the archives of horse and cattle history. Uncle Alfred was pleased with the results of the work and Charles decided to go back to Colorado, where he still owned land. He was at Fort Morgan until 1898, raising alfalfa and sugar beets. He also had a track and owned horses and cattle.

Here he met Alice Lowe, "the best woman scholar and teacher in all that section." Once he won a nice top buggy on a chance. He would hitch a pair of colts to the buggy and drive ten miles to the school where she was teaching so he could bring her home to Fort Morgan.

One day he was out driving with Alice when a hailstorm came up, so severe that hailstones came through the top of the buggy and pelted the colts. They bolted and ran away. Charles couldn't hold them and they ran over the plain until they tired themselves out.

He was on horseback on his way to Living Springs Ranch when word reached him that his uncle Alfred B. Darling had died. Riding hard, he managed to catch the train for New York City and arrived in time for the funeral.

In 1898, Charles and his young wife, Alice, settled permanently in Lyndonville. Their children were Charles M. Darling Jr., born August 10, 1899, and Caroline S., born September 12, 1900. Alice died in 1901 and later Charles married Mary McCauley, originally from the province of Quebec. They had four children: Velma, born February 28, 1903; Scott R., born March 12, 1904; Beatrice M., born August 11, 1905; and Alfred B., born April 22, 1910. Beatrice married Dr. Phillip Ransom and Caroline married Harold Ahearn. Alfred bought and ran the Darling Hotel in Lyndonville for a time.

Their father, Charles M., was a prominent figure around Lyndonville. He was a community supporter, serving as president and director of the old Lyndonville fairs, which discontinued in 1900. Charles helped to start them again in 1933, and these community fairs continue even today. Since 1938 it has been known as the Caledonia County Fair and has been held at the Lyndonville fairgrounds each year. Charles was an active member of the Lyndonville Driving Club and also served a term or two as village trustee. He dealt in real estate, land, cattle and horses. His house was on the corner of Main and Center Streets and one of his barns on Center Street is still there. He served a term in legislature and in 1917 was appointed forest fire warden for the town of Lyndon, serving for a number of years.

Back row: Flavia Folsom, niece; Charles M. Darling; *front row*: Charles M. Darling Jr., Scott, Alfred, Carolyn.

Charles M. looked forward to the winter horse racing that the Lyndonville Driving Club sponsored for many years. Main Street was the quarter-mile "speedway." Stores and businesses closed on Saturday afternoons so everyone could watch these exciting events that called the attention of Boston papers, *Life* magazine and many other noteworthy media. These winter events ended each year with a big finale on Washington's Birthday and a banquet that evening for the club. There were speakers and entertainment, bets paid off and trophies awarded. In 1938, the banquet was held at the Darling Inn and Charles M. Darling, the "Grand Old Man of harness racing," was pictured on the front of the souvenir menu with his horse Nina Dillon.

John B. Chase reported in his *Vermont Union-Journal* that year that it was most exciting to see Herbert Rugg, eighty-six, of Lowell, Massachusetts, and Charles M. Darling, eighty-one, of Lyndonville, racing their horses. "They came down the speedway in a race of four heats and then were at the evening banquet as fit and lively as any present."

Before the fairs were started up again on the old trotting park not far from my home, horsemen would jog their horses by our house to exercise them. It was about a two- or three-mile jog from Lyndonville, by our farm and around to Lyndonville again. One day I heard a big, strange noise as a horse jogged by our house. My mother said, "Oh, that is Charlie Darling. He just sneezed." Everyone knew his unusually hearty sneeze. One day when I was working in Lyndonville Bank, one of the workers sneezed. Mr. Riley, head of the bank, happened into the workroom just then. "Are you trying to rival Charlie Darling?" he asked, laughing. But the teasing was in fun. He, along with about everyone else, respected Mr. Darling.

Charles Darling died December 23, 1944. He and his family are buried in Lyndon Center.

Alfred Burbank Darling

Alfred Burbank Darling, Ebenezer's third son, was born March 22, 1821. In a large family, it was the custom of the time for boys, as soon as they could help, to augment the family income. When Alfred was fourteen he went to live with his uncle Timothy Fisher near Burke Green, in the center of the town of Burke. Timothy could no doubt use the help of another boy on the farm, as his children were all girls except one. Girls could do the work of cooking, spinning, weaving, sewing, soap making and a great many things, while the men and boys did the heavy farm work to earn the family living.

Alfred grew up like a brother with his cousins, the young Fishers—Edwin, Susan, Pamela, Roxana, Matilda and Emily. They attended the White School, named not for its color, but because the school stood on land that was once owned by Elam White. Alfred was remembered as a studious boy, especially good at arithmetic, always "doing sums." Once he got a whipping in school for spelling subtraction "subs-traction." His skill with figures, as we shall see, turned out to be a blessing for his future career.

The two boys, Alfred and Edwin, got into mischief. Squire Fisher had forbidden them to sugar off while boiling sap at the sugar place. But Edwin "hooked" his mother's lard kettle, so the story goes, carried it to the sugar camp and they had themselves some sweet feasts. Mrs. Fisher missed the kettle but had no idea where it was because the boys had hidden it in a barrel of soft soap in an outhouse. The next winter she found it when she scraped the bottom of the barrel. "Dipping soap with my fat kettle!" she exclaimed in disgust. "Just like one of Susan's capers." The story ends here, but one can imagine the boys' delight in escaping the blame. Sometimes the story is told a little differently, but this is the way it was told by Charles T. Walter in the *St. Johnsbury Republican*, Burke Centennial Edition, July 1, 1896.

Alfred continued to work for his uncle on the farm and turn his wages over to his father. Because Alfred was faithful to his work on the farm, his uncle Timothy Fisher had such a high regard for his nephew that he thought to deed the farm to him in return for Alfred's care so long as he, Timothy, lived. A light twist of fate changed the whole course of Alfred's life.

A young A.B. Darling, from a tintype.

How did Alfred, a country lad, come to achieve fame and fortune in the hotel business? On a trip to Boston with his uncle Timothy and teams loaded with produce, they stopped at a tavern in Charlestown Neck. The proprietor took such a liking to this young Alfred that he persuaded him to come to work for him. This inn was established by James Sullivan, promoter of the American Revolution and in 1807 governor of Massachusetts. It was a noted and favorite hostelry.

Alfred did leave his uncle's farm and went to work at the inn, where he stayed for over two years, learning every detail as faithfully as he had on his uncle's farm. Here he began to form plans that he steadfastly followed and that made him one of the most famous hotel proprietors of the world. After two and a half years, he must have decided it was time to begin to put his plans to work.

With six dollars in his pocket, so the story goes, Alfred went to Boston, where he applied for a job with Paran Stevens, a noted hotel landlord of the times. Mr. Stevens gave him a job in the hall (as a bellboy) at the Revere House, the best hotel in the city. That was a good start, a foot in the door, so to speak.

"Pleased with the boy," as Charles M. Chase, editor of the Lyndon weekly the *Vermont Union* wrote, "Mr. Stevens soon moved the young lad to the dining hall. He did so well that he was soon made waiter, and it wasn't long before Mr. Stevens promoted Alfred to purchasing agent for the whole establishment."

The *Boston Sunday Globe* of February 24, 1907, put it this way:

> *The third son of Ebenezer Darling was named Alfred Burbank Darling. This quiet studious boy, excelling in arithmetic, laid the firm foundation and acquired in great part, the fortune of the house of Darling. When he was 21 he arrived in Boston with only a few dollars in his pocket. The Revere House was then the finest hotel in the city, and the people of Burke like to tell how Alfred secured a position there as bellboy, then later became waiter and afterward chief steward. In time he developed so fine a capacity for management, both in financial and domestic departments of a large hotel that when the manager, Paran Stevens, went into the famous Battle House at Mobile, Ala., he took Mr. Darling into partnership. When the Civil War broke out they came north, and Mr. Stevens leased the Fifth Avenue Hotel which was then uncompleted. Under the direction of Hitchcock, Darling & Co. (composed of Paran Stevens, A.B. Darling, and Hiram Hitchcock), it was completed and opened in 1859.*

The Fifth Avenue Hotel was built to be the best hotel in New York City, if not the United States. Stevens, Darling and Hitchcock became the proprietors. Darling and Hitchcock were not wealthy and incurred some risk in sinking their small savings into this large venture. The Fifth Avenue Hotel was far uptown, beyond the usual "grand rush" of current business. The proprietors, however, took note of the tendency of the times, correctly, it turned out, and made everything first class in spite of the expense. As editor Chase wrote, "[the business] soon turned the current of wealthy travel, business and political, up town into the Fifth Avenue Hotel." The hotel enjoyed great success for more than forty years.

In the meantime Alfred B. Darling married Lydia Nye of Boston. They had no children. They lived in Madison Square, New York City, spending their summers at their handsome estate, Darlington, in Ramsey, New Jersey. Darlington was a beautiful country estate with fine horses, carriages, registered Jersey cattle and lovely, well-kept gardens, "all the things," states his biographer, Mabel Hall Walter, in 1896, "that he dreamed of when he was a poor boy in Burke, Vermont."

Mrs. Darling had come from Auburndale, Massachusetts, and probably through her influence, Alfred bought a large comfortable estate there and organized a small boarding school for boys. Dr. Cushing, an old friend of his from East Burke, was the headmaster and about fourteen boys from Lyndon and Burke attended sometime during the years. One was Alfred's nephew from Lyndon, Charles M. Darling, and another nephew Lucius A. Darling from Burke.

Alfred never forgot his native town and the church where he was baptized and received as a member during his early youth. He bought the Baptist church in East Burke and presented it to the Congregational Society in memory of his father and mother. He was chief contributor to the repairs and upkeep of the old meetinghouse at Burke Hollow, as well as the "Old White Schoolhouse" that was moved to East Burke and maintained as a museum. In New York City, he had an interest in the growing city and was director of several banks and a member of prominent clubs. He and his partners became members of the Chestnut Hill Land Company and helped create the Mount Vernon development, a beautiful residential area.

In the Burke Centennial issue of the *St. Johnsbury Republican*, editor Walter wrote that Alfred Darling was a "man of well-balanced impulses, generous and of authoritative presence." It is said of him, "His word is worth a pound where the word of others weighs nothing."

Alfred, unfortunately, sustained a serious shock from which he did not recover when he was thrown from a carriage while driving near his country home at Ramsey, New Jersey. He died September 6, 1896. His funeral was at 15 Madison Square North on September 10 with his pastor, the Reverend E. Stimpson, officiating. The burial was at Woodlawn Cemetery in New

A.B. Darling.

York, where he owned a lot on which rests a beautiful sarcophagus. Most of his estate went to nieces and nephews, and in particular, his interest in the Fifth Avenue Hotel went to his nephew Elmer. After Alfred died in 1896, his widow disposed of the farm to Elmer A. Darling, who sold it to George Crocker, a banker in New York. Elmer brought part of the Jersey herd to Mountain View Farm.

Lydia Nye Darling lived until February 28, 1903.

The Fifth Avenue Hotel

The history of the Fifth Avenue Hotel where Alfred Darling and his nephew Elmer made their fortunes is a fascinating story. A 1929 Arnold Constable ad celebrating its 102nd anniversary reported, "In 1837 when Fifth Avenue was being extended north of 24th Street, the Horn farmhouse stood in the path of the new thoroughfare. Two years later it was moved to the corner of Fifth Avenue and 23rd Street and converted to a tavern known as 'The Madison Cottage' where gay young blades and conscientious drinkers gathered."

Arnold Constable's was "A Great Fifth Avenue Store" where Mrs. Abraham Lincoln and Mrs. Ulysses Grant often shopped. The store, a large impressive building, occupied an entire block at Canal, Mercer and Howard Streets. In the early days there were no stores on Fifth Avenue.

But Fifth Avenue was soon to be "the place." In 1844, Madison Square, named for President Madison, was formally opened. In another few years Fifth Avenue was growing in length, beauty and prestige, and people began building fine houses there.

Madison Cottage, where "no more than 5 persons shall sleep in a bed," was torn down in 1852, and in 1859 Amos Eno built the Fifth Avenue Hotel on the site. Located on Madison Square at the intersection of Fifth Avenue and Broadway, the Fifth Avenue Hotel was pretty far "uptown" in those days, away from the center of activity. It was laughingly nicknamed "Eno's Folly," but the skeptical and amused people were wrong. This hotel became the hub of New York's social and political life.

It was six stories high, had gas lighting and boasted a new contraption, a "vertical railway" (spelled "verticle" in the ad). Eno could boast of this new contraption because Elisha Graves Otis, a former Vermonter with plenty of Vermont ingenuity, now of Yonkers, New York, had already demonstrated an elevator with a safety device, his invention, at the New York City Fair in 1854. The first passenger elevator was installed in the city in 1857. Otis invented a device that would prevent the car from falling if the ropes broke, which they often did with the old steam-powered elevators. The hotel claimed it to be the first passenger elevator ever put in successful operation in this country.

Madison Cottage was torn down in 1852, and the Fifth Avenue Hotel was built on the site.

Fifth Avenue Hotel.

The Prince of Wales came to the Fifth Avenue Hotel in 1860 and the traveler who came with him said the hotel was "both a larger and handsomer building than Buckingham Palace," according to "The Fifth Avenue Hotel and New York City Life," Michael S. Freeman's article in *Heritage Magazine of the New York Historical Association*, 1989. A crowd estimated to be 150,000 crowded the sidewalks from Castle Garden, where he landed, to the hotel to catch a glimpse of the prince pass by in his scarlet coat and white plumed hat.

General Grant, the great hero of the Civil War, came to New York in November 1865. The reception and dinner given for him at the Fifth Avenue Hotel was underestimated. The halls, parlors and stairways were so jammed with people that many never got to see the general and Mrs. Grant at all, or the Generals Wood, Cook and Hooker who were with them at the reception.

By 1879, Madison Square Garden occupied the abandoned New York and Harlem railroad depot, until architect Stanford White designed the new Madison Square Garden in 1890 on the same site. People coming to the Fifth Avenue Hotel may have looked to see which way the wind was blowing by the direction Augustus St. Gaudens's Diana, the best-known weather vane in the world, was turning atop Madison Square Garden. It was replaced by a second Diana in 1893; she was a slimmer figure and was better placed on the dome. When this Madison Square Garden was torn down in 1925, Diana was stored in a Brooklyn warehouse for seven years until she finally found a home in the Philadelphia Museum of Art.

Some said the Fifth Avenue Hotel was the ultimate in tasteful luxury; others thought of it as overheated, overupholstered and overfitted with mechanical devices. In her novelette *New Year's Day*, Edith Wharton wrote that the hotel was frequented by "politicians" and "Westerners." Nevertheless, in spite of these criticisms, which were not confined to the Fifth Avenue Hotel alone, and were not everyone's opinion, this was one of the great hotels of its day.

Because this part of the city had grown so much, an ad in the *New York Tribune* on May 26, 1898, could boast,

> *It is in the very heart of the shopping district and easily accessible to art galleries and amusements and has direct car communication with all railways and important points. American and European Plans. American Plan at the highest standard of excellence. Terms $5.00 per day and upwards, including steam heat or open fires. The European Plan will have every possible resources and convenience for those who prefer that plan. Terms for rooms $2.00 per day and upwards, including steam heat or open fires.*

The ad said that the hotel was less than ten minutes by electric car to the New York Central, Harlem and New Haven Railroads, and twenty-three minutes to the Twenty-third and Twenty-fourth Street ferries. At first outgoing trains were drawn by horses from there to the place where Grand Central Station was later built.

The Amen Corner

For more than forty years the Fifth Avenue Hotel was the headquarters for the Republican State Committee and was identified with numerous notable local and national events and claimed many noted guests, such as the Prince of Wales, King Edward VII, presidents, senators, generals and admirals.

The political as well as the social life of the city gravitated to this "last word in luxury hotels." Supposedly eleven presidents have sat on the plush benches of the "Amen Corner"—Grant, Hayes, Garfield, Arthur, Cleveland, Harrison, McKinley, Roosevelt, Taft, Wilson and Harding. President Cleveland made the hotel his headquarters, according to the *New York Herald Tribune* of Sunday, September 25, 1925.

The hotel's broad, spacious corridor opened directly onto Broadway and Fifth Avenue. Toward the rear of the hotel the corridor narrowed, forming two corners, which made an excellent place for meetings. When Senator Platt made the hotel his home, the familiar corner became the center of political activity. The political conferences held there came to be known as "Platt's Sunday School," a name coined by a *New York News* writer. Platt himself said that when a group came to a decision the crowd in that corner of the lobby would say "Amen."

Countless problems were discussed here and many a decision reached. The sofas or seats they sat on were made of cherry, then "the fashionable wood." They were so well made that only the upholstery had to be replaced from time to time. When the hotel was to be torn down, the furniture of the Amen Corner was preserved because "the famous seats had played an unique role in the politics of the state and nation for more than half a century," wrote the *New York Herald Tribune* on Sunday, September 13, 1925. The seats were much sought after, but all bids were refused and the four sofas were presented to the Amen Corner Corporation. Two were presented to the New York Historical Society, and the other two were carefully preserved and privately owned. But a fabulous hotel that was built in 1859 and considered too far uptown became too far out of town and was torn down in 1908.

FIFTH AVENUE HOTEL JAN. 27_1904.

The Amen Corner. Note the plush seats. *Cartoon by D. McCarthy, 1904.*

The Fifth Avenue Building was erected in 1909–10 on the site of the old Fifth Avenue Hotel, and another office building put up around 1940. The *New York Times* of December 3, 1958, announced the sale of this property with a rental area of 500,000 square feet, assessed at $6,612,000. The sale was made by the Eno heirs and the Fifth Avenue Building Company to a syndicate of investors.

A Day with Elmer Darling at the Fifth Avenue Hotel

Having gotten things rolling at Mountain View Farm under the management of his brother Lucius, this is a good time to find out just what Elmer's work entailed at the Fifth Avenue Hotel in New York City.

Editor of the *Vermont Union* Charles M. Chase, traveling south in 1887, stopped at the Fifth Avenue Hotel on his way, being assured by the conductor on the Boston & Albany that the "Fifth Avenue Hotel was a well-kept tavern." In his report Chase commented, "I find the hotel with only two proprietors even better than the St. Johnsbury House with seventeen."

This visit written up in Mr. Chase's weekly paper, the *Vermont Union*, back home in Lyndon, not only gives an account of how a local "boy" was making good in the big city, but also tells what it took to run a big city hotel. By the time Chase made his visit, Elmer was in charge of market buying, keeping account of all expenses as well as being private secretary to his uncle Alfred's business, including his fancy stock farm (in Ramsey, New Jersey), which Chase said, "makes a convenient ventilator for his large hotel income."

Elmer would rise at six o'clock in the morning and find out from steward A.G. Thompson the number of guests in the house. A hack would be waiting for him at the door, in which he rode to market to purchase the supplies for the day from the list made out by the steward.

Elmer's average purchases for the day would include 140 dozen eggs, 170 pounds of butter, 525 quarts of milk, 80 quarts of cream and 4,000 oysters, besides meat, fish, poultry, fruit and vegetables the steward had listed. Delicacies would include duck, turtle and terrapin. Other supplies not purchased every day would include flour, salt, sugar, soap, barrels of charcoal and whatever else was needed to run a fine hotel. From 1859 to 1886, the books showed $8 million spent for marketing. "Quite a business, you see," commented Mr. Chase.

There was bound to be waste when there were as many as fifty-two items to choose from for breakfast and seventy-five dishes for dinner. Every day a man with a cart would take away a load of "broken victuals," which he

Right: From left: E.A. Darling, Charles Vilas, A.B. Darling and Hiram Hitchcock.

Below: The front of the Fifth Avenue Hotel menu cover.

could sell for a discount to poor people and for which he paid the hotel $140 a month. The hog man would pick up the swill (bits of bread, meat, poultry, fish, cheese, pie and fruit), for which he paid the hotel $1,000 a year. The hotel received $2,000 a year for grease left over after scrubbing soap was made for the hotel's own use.

"I am indebted to Mr. Darling for a complete inspection of the inside working of his hotel," Chase wrote. They started at the receiving room in the basement and followed through all the departments. There was $2,000 worth of beef ripening in the refrigerator. The kitchen was supplied with a twenty-five-foot range, two immense brick ovens and a roasting corner where numerous roasts of beef, pork, poultry and game were constantly revolving. The large kitchen was full of workers, meat cooks, pastry cooks, griddlecake makers and others; everything was in a system and no one was in another one's way. Ferrand, the head cook, started there in 1859, as had the steward Thompson.

Loverin, the old porter who was also there from the beginning, was better known to the guests than the proprietors themselves. In 1887, when Chase made his trip, Loverin had handled the trunks daily for twenty-eight years and knew where all the owners hailed from. The man at the cigar case had been there for sixteen years, and Frank, brother of Sam Moore of St. Johnsbury, had fifteen years behind the Fifth Avenue bar and his department was as neat as a ladies' parlor. Besides hall boys, waiters, cooks, chambermaids and door boys, there were one or more painters, carpenters, masons, plumbers, frescoers, upholsterers, cabinetmakers and others in constant employ.

Chase wrote, "It isn't every man can keep a hotel, but Darling has proved a conspicuous success, putting money in his purse, reflecting credit upon his family name and honor upon his native town."

The average 375 guests a day paid at that time five dollars a day, which included meals with five settings daily. The hotel was occupied by many boarders, even families, who for an extra dollar or so per day received an adjoining bath. Lodgers could afford to live in the hotel and do away with the problems of maintaining a home and the tiresome housekeeping or hiring of servants.

Mountain View Farm

*T*his farm was established in 1883 by Elmer A. Darling (1848–1931), a native of East Burke, who became part owner/manager of the world famous Fifth Avenue Hotel in New York City. After the hotel closed in 1908, Mr. Darling retired to the life of a gentleman farmer and raised prize-winning Morgan horses and Jersey cattle. The farm also produced the choice "Darling" brand of cheeses and butter. At its zenith, his prosperous Mountain View Farm included Burke Mountain and extended over 7,000 acres.

The farm's monumental barns and distinctive colonial yellow and white-trimmed farmhouses line Darling Hill Road. Elmer Darling studied architecture at M.I.T. and with assistance of Jardine, Kent and Jardine Architects designed his magnificent neo-Georgian residence, Burklyn Hall. Built in 1905–1908 on a knoll astride the Burke/Lyndon town line. Mr. Darling was a public-spirited citizen whose philanthropic generosity includes the Colonial Revival style Burke Mountain Club built in East Burke in 1910. Vermont Division for Historic Preservation—1998.

This Historic Preservation sign is posted by the roadside at the Inn at Mountain View Farm in the town of Burke today. It is one of many such signs all around the Green Mountain State's many places that stand in proud recognition of its noted people and places of historic value.

Elmer Albert Darling was born April 22, 1848, on the farm his father Henry carved out of the forest near the foot of Burke Mountain. He must have gone to school in Sutton because the family moved to a farm there in 1854. In 1866 they came back and lived in the house in East Burke village. Elmer went to St. Johnsbury Academy, and because there is particular mention of "during the tenure of Professor Colby," he must have been an influence on Elmer's schooling. Elmer, interested in architecture, went to MIT (Massachusetts Institute of Technology) for a specialized course. He taught school in Burke for a few terms and then, around 1872, he went to New York City to work for his Uncle Alfred in the Fifth Avenue Hotel.

Mountain View Farm. *From* Successful Vermonters, *1904.*

It must have been a red-letter day when Elmer bought the Harley Hall farm located upon the ridge southwest of East Burke village in 1873. Henry advised his son Elmer to buy this farm, and it was well he heeded this advice because it was the start of the fabulous Mountain View Farm. When all repairs and renovations were done, the family moved up from East Burke Village. Elmer thought they would enjoy the more spacious house and the wonderful views of Burke Mountain and the countryside. There was one great barn at Mountain View Farm, and it was not long before Elmer added more very well-constructed Connecticut Valley–style barns.

Beginning at the foot of the long ridge road at Lyndon near Folsom's Crossing, Elmer began buying up other farms and cabins along this road. He had a desire to do what he could to restore the old buildings and add more land to the 800 acres he already owned at Mountain View Farm. The farms he bought were the Hall place, 350 acres; the Jenkins place known as the old Lemuel Walter farm, 170 acres; the Belden farm, about 180 acres; the Amidon place in 1888, 72 acres; meadow from Thomas Fairbrother, 10 acres; and woodland and pasture from Dr. Abel Brown in 1894, 125 acres. Elmer also bought a timber lot of 112 acres.

Elmer's study of architecture gave him the ability to see what these places could look like. He drew plans for repairs and renovations. Since his own work was at the Fifth Avenue Hotel, Elmer put his younger brother Lucius in charge of carrying out the plans with local carpenters and builders. One large house was renovated into a boardinghouse for workers who needed a place to stay.

Though their father, Henry, was physically infirm, he was mentally alert, and with his experience from his pioneering days and all the knowledge he had acquired through his years, he could offer advice and suggestions. Suggestions and advice from Henry, the capable supervision of Lucius and the money coming from Elmer in New York gave this hill a whole new look and work for a lot of people.

Old cellar holes and foundations were filled in and smoothed over to open up fertile fields and pastures. Land was leveled and graded and fences were repaired or done away with. Some old houses were torn down and replaced. Plans for the great farm included planting maple trees and making many more available for sugaring by clearing underbrush from the woodlands. Elmer owned thirty-four houses and rented them to families, most of whom worked at Mountain View Farm.

West of the creamery is a carriage house and beyond that the piggery, a small, well-ventilated house with six pens and an arch where the mash is prepared. The last building in the row is a bull barn. It contains three pens and here is kept a noble Jersey bull that was purchased at the Burnhan stock farm in Saugatuck, near Bridgeport, Connecticut.

Behind the large barn there is also a house for storing the farm implements, with wagon sheds underneath. Here are kept two large machines, two sulky plows, a corn planter, grain seeder, ball bearing mowing machine, harvester and Osborn horse rake, besides the harrows, plows and other tools necessary on a large farm. There were cow barns, horse barns, carriage barns and hay barns, all with "gracefully wrought weather vanes turning in the wind. All these stables and barns are kept sweet and clean with fresh sawdust in the stables, all litter from the hay and straw swept out and even the cobwebs chased away."

There are two sugar places containing a total of 1,900 trees, all of which have been fitted with modern apparatus. The product is mostly maple syrup that is consumed in the Fifth Avenue Hotel.

When they were restored or rebuilt, all buildings were painted yellow with white trim. The original names were not forgotten, because every yard had a handsome sign giving the name of the former owners, such as Howland, Belden, Bemis and so on.

The local people kept a close eye on the interesting things that were happening at Mountain View Farm. A newspaper clipping in the *Vermont Union* in December 1896 tells us that "E.A. Darling of New York city is here this week taking his agricultural bearings. A new horse barn 117 feet long has been completed at Mountain View Farm making with the others the finest set of farm buildings in northern Vermont. This farm enterprise is Mr. Darling's pet and we hope to add on his profit, but at present he makes more money in the Fifth Avenue Hotel."

The clock was installed by Charles H. Howe, Jane (Howe) Cameron's grandfather.

The idea was, I suppose, that editor Charles M. Chase thought of Elmer's farm as a hobby, since he was already making good money in New York City. But it appears that Elmer, whatever he undertook, was a benefit not only himself but also to everybody around the area. No doubt he had an idea that someday he would come back to his love, Burke Mountain, and the beautiful surroundings.

In June 1896 the *Union* says that the Mountain View herd of cattle had been increased by seven choice Jerseys from the herd of Mr. Hiram Hitchcock of Hanover, New Hampshire.

> *The Mountain View herd now ranks among the best in this whole section, additions being constantly made to it. Mountain View itself, with its elegant house, immense barns, sheds and other buildings, presents the appearance of a "city set on a hill." Not only is Mr. Darling to be congratulated on having such a farm in its boundaries, employing so many men who are well paid through the liberality of its owner. The estate now embraces the original large farm of the late Hon. Harley M. Hall, also the farms of William Belden, B.H. Jenkins, and C.C. Amidon. A visit to the place will amply repay any one who likes to inspect fine buildings, modern improvements and the best of stock.*

The Darling family home, Mountain View Farm. *Courtesy of the Inn at Mountain View Farm.*

It must have been a joy to Elmer whenever he came home from New York City, probably by train to the West Burke depot, to see how much had been done while his wishes were carried out under the supervision of his very capable brother Lucius. All this work and the running of the Mountain View Farm provided employment for hundreds of local families. The properties altogether became Mountain View Farm.

Elmer Helps Revitalize East Burke

S ettlement of the Burke township began when Lemuel Walter came from Litchfield, Connecticut, in 1792. In another year, several more families came and settled on the central ridge and land that grew into a little "village" called Burke Green. The settlers made application to Joseph Lord of St. Johnsbury, who issued the warning for the inhabitants to meet on September 5, 1796, for the purpose of organizing the town and electing officers. By 1801, the first school had been built near the center of town.

After 1815 there had been a rapid growth in population as more and more settlers came to Burke and settled lands. Farms prospered for a time, but winters were harsh. Typhoid, diphtheria, mumps, measles, scarlet fever and other diseases increased as the population increased. Then in 1842 an erysipelas epidemic ravaged Burke for six months, wiping out more than a fourth of the town's population. A flood in 1852 washed out sawmills, gristmills and homes along the Passumpsic River and mountain streams. "The settlers of Burke became discouraged and weary." Many joined the great western migration, so that by 1860 more than half the country's population had moved west of the Appalachians to Ohio, Indiana, Illinois and Kentucky.

Burke Green became desolate; only a few remained in the settlement and some of the farms on the ridge road were deserted and neglected. There were still some farms surrounding East Burke, but there was no railroad— the nearest railroad depot was some distance away in West Burke. There was no capital for developing industry. Sawmills and gristmills, blacksmith and harness shops saw only local use and there seemed no prospect for progress—until Elmer A. Darling bought the Harley Hall farm on the ridge, the site where Lemuel Walter had settled.

All the work on the buildings and constructing new barns on Elmer's properties gave the village of East Burke a big boost when he began restoring the mills and shops for needed lumber and many other things required in such work. He may not have started out to restore the little village, but what he did for his own dreams helped others realize theirs.

Elmer A. Darling acquired two mills on dams of the Passumpsic, one near Mount Hunger. Pipelines provided water up to the ridge to the Mountain

East Burke village, printed from a glass plate.

View Farm. He also made a small pond north of East Burke where ice could be harvested each winter.

In 1899, he bought the gristmill in East Burke and built a new dam and a dynamo to run water to Mountain View Farm for fire protection. This also ran machinery in the creamery that previously had been run by steam. He owned many houses in the village and supplied water and sewage for the whole village. When he built the electric plant, he gave the village streetlights. The plant was also an opportunity for those who wished to have lighting in their homes. He was instrumental in the village having concrete sidewalks. When the 1927 flood destroyed Elmer's electric plant in East Burke village, the Lyndonville Electric Department acquired the lines and supplied the electricity.

Elmer gave a lot of attention to Woodmont Cemetery in East Burke, transforming it from a little old burying ground into a beautiful cemetery. He bought additional land, built the Corinthian-style tomb and a tool house and set out trees. He enclosed the cemetery with a handsome iron fence with an entrance of stone pillars. He purchased a house for the sexton. Elmer did not do things halfway. Interest in the three cemeteries—Burke Hollow, Burke Green and Woodmont—as well as the old meetinghouse and the Congregational church were maintained by Elmer and Henry G. Darling II of Lyndonville.

His uncle Alfred of New York City had purchased a fairly new church in East Burke from the Baptists in 1865 for $1,800 and leased to the

The dam at East Burke that Elmer rebuilt.
From a glass plate.

Lucius and Margaret Darling's children,
Henry George II and Pearl Enid.

Congregational Society. When Alfred died, the church was left to the society in his will. Elmer renovated and decorated the church. The rounded ceiling was painted to resemble a sky with fleecy clouds. Elmer also purchased and fixed up a cottage, which he presented to the church for a parsonage with modern improvements.

For nine years, Lucius saw to it that all this was accomplished before he reached the age of thirty-five. He married Margaret McDonald of Burke and they moved into a fine house next door to the main house. Elmer made Lucius superintendent of all the operations of Mountain View Farm. Lucius and Margaret had two children—Pearl Enid, who died at age eight, and Henry George II, named for his grandfather.

Lucius A. Darling

Lucius A. Darling was born in Sutton on June 1, 1857. He was nine when the family moved back to East Burke and lived in the house his uncle Alfred had bought for his brother Henry's family. Lucius and his sister Louise then went to school in East Burke village. Lucius absorbed the town's history from stories his father told. Living in the center of the village, Lucius could "slip" down to Harris's store, where some of the men gathered at least once a day to talk about the town's and nation's affairs.

For a term or two, he attended Auburndale (the school his uncle Alfred had founded in Massachusetts), in addition to Lancaster New Hampshire Academy and Bryant and Stratton Business College in Boston. He worked as a carpenter for a time on Professor Henry Fairbanks's house and the North Church in St. Johnsbury.

Lucius was superintendent of Mountain View Farm in Burke and Lyndon for his brother Elmer. He handled all the business transactions and oversaw the hiring of help, erection of new buildings, repairing of old buildings, buying and selling of horses and cattle and overseeing of farm operations. In time he had a foreman, Fred Corliss, who assisted him, and later another foreman was Frank Stoddard. Lucius lived on the former Harley Hall place, which the family called home.

The *Child's Gazetteer* of 1887 lists Lucius Darling as follows: "E. Burke, r.45, 42 thoroughbred Jersey and Devon cattle, 51 head registered, 32 grade Cotswold sheep, 2 Morgan brood mares, Chester white swine, 700 sugar trees, supt. of stock farm owned by Elmer A. Darling of new York City."

Lucius was a community-minded citizen, and in spite of all his duties he still found time for public service. In 1900 he represented Burke in the legislature and in 1912 he was a state senator from Caledonia County. He was town selectman for twelve years, and for several years was chairman of the Republican Town Committee. He was also president of the Burke Mountain Club, trustee of the Woodmont Cemetery Association and he succeeded his brother Elmer as a director of the Lyndonville Savings Banks and Trust Company. He was the only surviving member of the old Burke Meetinghouse.

Left: Lucius Darling.

Below: Lucius could "slip" down to Harris's store and listen to what the men gathered there were discussing.

Lucius was thoughtful of others and when he started driving that "new-fangled contraption," the automobile, he would stop when he met a skittish horse, get out and lead the horse by his auto, earning the gratitude of the driver of the horse. One day he met an older couple in a buggy and noted that not only was the horse skittish, but the lady was taking on as well. Lucius stopped the auto and offered to lead the horse by. The man replied, "You lead the old lady by and I'll take care of the horse!"

When Elmer died in 1931, Lucius inherited the property in Burke to do with whatever he felt best. For several years he continued the operations. Lucius and his son Henry II were elected to settle Elmer's considerable estate, with property in New York City as well as Burke. In his will, Elmer left some of his wealth to his brother Lucius and his sister Louise, and the rest was for generous public bequests.

Everything in Burke was well taken care of and Lucius and his family spent a number of weeks in the sunny south. The *St. Petersburg Times* of February 4, 1932, reported,

> *Vermont People Enjoy Visit. Coming from what they claim is the prettiest state in the north to what is claimed the prettiest state in the southland, Mr. and Mrs. L.A. Darling, East Burke, Vt., are enjoying an extended visit at the DeVille hotel. They reached here several weeks ago and are accompanied by their son Henry Darling and Mrs. Darling's sister, Miss Lilla McDonald, also of Vermont.*
>
> *Speaking of his native state, Darling told of his extensive land properties, comprising approximately 9,000 acres. The main farmland on which they live, consists of 2,600 acres, and includes Burke Mountain which rises to an elevation of 3,500 feet. So proud of the mountain of East Burke that they are building an automobile road to the summit. This, Darling added, would be a great drawing card for the tourists who pass through part of Vermont which, by the way is only 35 miles from the Canadian border line.*
>
> *Mr. and Mrs. Darling and the others in the group plan to be at the DeVille several weeks longer and upon their return trip north will motor by way of the east coast.*

In 1933, Lucius and his son Henry decided together to give the vast landholdings over the mountain to the state of Vermont. The property became the Darling State Forest Park. In 1936, Lucius sold Burklyn Hall and properties to the south of it to Earle Brown, who operated it as a showplace for a number of years. He had Belgian horses and many people remember the beautiful teams pulling the handsome huge wagon in the cavalcade at the Caledonia County Fair in Lyndonville.

Lucius A. Darling died February 15, 1937, and his wife Margaret McDonald Darling died January 27, 1952. They are buried in the family lot at Woodmont Cemetery in East Burke.

The Bear Story

A bear wandering around Mountain View Farm might pose a threat to some of the animals. This story is all written on the back of a photograph. The date and the author are not given.

> *Mr. Darling* [Lucius] *was walking across the pasture with the stick as a cane, met the bear but neither stopped to pick a quarrel. Mr. Darling came to village and telephoned on to hill that he had met the bear and the direction he was going when he last saw him. Then telephones got busy and they chased Mr. Bear across the field and he headed for the mountainside, in attempting to cross the mill pond was at mercy of gun fire from both sides the pond. He succeeded in getting across and started up Dish Mill brook when someone fired the fatal bullet. Think there were twenty-five bullets in him when he was dressed off for the taxidermist. The only near fatality other than the Bear was the piece out of the rim of Ira Hunter's hat where a shot went wild across the mill pond.*

The picture shows several men with their hands raised holding up the pole from which Mr. Bear is hanging. The men in the photograph are listed from left to right: "Am not sure of first man, may be from Lyndonville, second, Dr. Dwinell, Scott Stafford end of pole, think the next was Daigle from Victory Road, Charlie Foster, Alvah Gilson, Harry Simms, men each side of the Bear were working for Mr. Darling, Jake Jock, George Gilson, Ira Hunter, Ora Jenkins, Mr. Lucius Darling [the man wearing vest], Dr. Root, Ed Harvey, Mr. James, Charlie Freeto."

After it served as a prize for many years and graced a floor at Mountain View Farm as a rug, eventually, as bearskin rugs will do, it became moth eaten and was shedding. So it was done away with, but not before placing first in an Easter parade at Burke Mountain when it skied down the mountain—draped over the head of a skier.

Old Schoolhouse Is Saved

Elmer Darling may have been busy with his work at the Fifth Avenue Hotel in New York City, but he always helped keep things going in Burke too. In 1895 Elmer, Mrs. Mary V. Belden, Mrs. Mabel Walter and others formed the Society for the Study of the History of Burke. The name was changed later to the more convenient title of the Burke Historical Society. What spurred this group into action was the closing of the old White School in 1894.

The schoolhouse was situated about halfway between the families living near the first settlement on the ridge and the green. It stood at the crossroads of Pinkham Road, east toward the mountain, and the long hill over the iron bridge leading to the green and on to Burke Hollow. It burned in 1817. The next year a new school was built of heavy timbers, presumably from the sawmill nearby. Although it was painted red, the school was called the White School because it stood on land that was formerly part of Elam White's farm.

In the spring of 1894 the last term in the school was taught by Inez Humphrey. The schoolhouse, about two and a half miles north of East Burke village, was offered for sale, but this group of historic-minded citizens, interested in preserving the history of Burke, formed the Burke Historical Society and set out to save it.

The desks, designed for several children to sit at each one, were built on a raised platform around the room, perhaps to keep little feet off cold floors. The backrests were high and straight. The desks had narrow slant tops and two shelves underneath, and show marks of busy jackknives,

At floor level, the front part of the desks formed backrests for additional benches around the room. These were no doubt for recitation work or possibly overflow of children, as there had been as many as seventy-five pupils at once. The teacher's desk was the same as the others and was built in one front corner. A teacher seated there commanded full view of the room.

This arrangement left the center of the room empty, perhaps for better chance for heat from the fireplace to circulate to all corners. There was

An old one-room school makes a great museum.

certainly no loss of heat through the solid walls, the heavy plank door or the many high windows. One wonders how much heat penetrated the solid desks to the feet and legs of the children. However, it must be remembered that our sturdy Vermont ancestors dressed for the times in warm woolen clothing. Later a shed and entry room were added, and in 1849 the fireplace was removed because box stoves had come into more common use.

In 1923 the old White Schoolhouse was uprooted, placed on skids and drawn over the snow-covered roads by several pairs of horses. The two-and-a-half-mile trip was a hazardous one, taking a day and a half. Once on a downhill grade the schoolhouse "got away" and slid into the horses, injuring one so badly that he had to be killed.

Finally reaching its destination, the lawn of the Burke Mountain Clubhouse, the building received minor repairs and a new stain. A fireplace was added to the entry room so it could be furnished to represent an old-time kitchen. The schoolroom, however, was kept the same, except for the display of antiques and Burke historical relics too numerous to mention. These were donated by many residents, past and present, who were interested in passing and sharing their historical heritage.

The globe of the world made by Peter Curtis Newell in Burke in 1800 still stands on the teacher's desk. On the wall hang the original blackboard and a hand-drawn colored map of the United States, which includes the territories of the west.

Under the protective care of the Burke Mountain Club and the Burke Historical Society, the old school museum stands in a colorful Vermont setting waiting for visitors who stop for a glimpse into the past.

Henry G. Darling II

Henry George Darling II, born August 13, 1898, went to school in East Burke, Lyndon Institute and then on to Worcester (Massachusetts) Academy. Later he attended Bryant and studied business administration at the Stratton Commercial School in Boston.

While Henry was growing up, his grandfather (also named Henry) was still living next door at Mountain View Farm, and Louise was still living there as well. Henry II "spent happy hours," said Mabel Walter, "listening to all of the humorous and exciting stories of escapades and experiences of early days in Burke, still vital and bright in Grandfather's memory." Henry could remember his grandfather and his own father, Lucius, continued the tradition and the stories lived on.

Henry II was about four when his grandfather died, but he worked and played on the farm and his father Lucius kept the stories of his father's generation alive. Many a day young Henry trudged to the summit of Burke Mountain when his father was building the first fire tower up there. He skated on the ice pond and was familiar with the gristmills and the power mills. He was also at home in the huge barns and extensive gardens. It was an ideal childhood with beautiful horses and carriages on hand. There was so much for a boy to watch with "so many busy men and women accomplishing exciting and interesting things."

Henry II was associated with his uncle Elmer Darling in real estate and banking. After his uncle's death in 1931, Henry II returned to his home at Mountain View Farm and continued his business from there. When his Uncle Elmer died, Henry and his father Lucius were elected to settle the vast estate with property in New York City as well as Burke and the area.

Henry assisted his father Lucius in the administration of the Darling estates in Burke, collecting rents and managing renovations and repairs. Offices in New York City were maintained until the estate was settled. This also included much of Alfred Darling's estate in New Jersey. To take care of all this, Henry spent much time traveling back and forth between New York City and Burke.

Left: Henry George Darling II.

Below: Henry, seated in middle front, at school in East Burke village.

Right: This may not be a Morgan, but Henry seems to enjoy a good ride on this horse.

Below: Henry with his dog; the name of the dog is unknown today.

DARLING'S MORGANS
EAST BURKE.VT

Fred Davis takes Henry for a sleigh ride with a handsome pair of Morgans.

Lucius and Henry decided together to give the vast landholdings over on the mountain to the state of Vermont. These 1,750 acres of forest and field on the mountain became the Darling State Forest Park. They added the stone house at the gateway and about 28 more acres to the park. This included some of the old homestead of Henry's grandfather, Henry Darling I.

Lucius and Henry II made an agreement with the town of Burke to pay 50 percent of the cost of work that was badly needed in the Burke Hollow and Burke Green Cemeteries. Stones that had toppled over were reset, fill was brought, grading and seeding were done and fences were repaired. Henry also took on the books of the Woodmont Cemetery in East Burke and was president of the association for many years.

Henry was a trustee vice-president of Lyndonville Savings Band and Trust Company and a trustee of Lyndon Institute. He was a member of the Morgan Horse Club and Jersey Cattle Club. He served in the legislature for Caledonia County in 1939–40.

He married Kathleen Chaffee of St. Johnsbury Center on September 19, 1941, and they lived at Mountain View Farm until they moved to a house on Center Street in Lyndonville, formerly the home of Harley and Jennie (Darling) Folsom.

When I was working with the Friends of Burklyn, I went to see Mr. Darling in Lyndonville a couple of times for research. He was very gracious and seemed pleased to talk about whatever I asked him, whether it be his uncle Elmer, the Morgan horses or Mountain View Farm.

The snowshoe party ready to go. Henry is sitting on the running board.

A snowshoe party, 1913. Henry is third from left. Maybe the dog was shy of the camera.

One time I was asking about Elmer's motor launch, the *Burklyn*, he'd had at Lake Willoughby. Henry described it with great detail. I also talked to the young men who then owned it. I even drove over to Shelburne Bay near Burlington, Vermont, to have a look at it myself. It was under a tarp, but I was able to get underneath to have a good look at the things Henry had described to me so I could depict them in an article I wrote. I looked for the things Henry Darling described, particularly the brass fittings and the etched glass doors on the cupboards.

It appears that the description of Elmer Darling fits his nephew Henry Darling II as well: dignified, somewhat shy, with a great sense of humor. He enjoyed telling the stories that were handed down by the Darlings from generation to generation. He had a great appreciation and respect for the family traditions.

The Boulders at Willoughby Lake

Elmer Darling owned two cottages at the bend of the road near the south end of Willoughby Lake. In 1914, he turned the cottage known as Sunset View over to the Lyndonville Village Improvement Society (VIS), rent-free. It was to be used as a tearoom to raise funds for maintenance of the several parks in Lyndonville. He retained one cottage, Cragmere, and the motor launch for his own use. Later he improved the tearoom by adding paneling and a fireplace.

In 1921 he built the Boulders dance casino, which he also turned over to the VIS rent-free for fundraising. The opening dance on Tuesday, August 3, 1921, in the new casino was a huge success, with 475 people attending. The gaily lit buildings and the moonlight shining through the trees on the water helped make the evening memorable. Dr. F.H. Davis, on behalf of the society, expressed appreciation to Mr. Darling for his "kind act." Mr. Darling spoke about building the casino and said he was pleased to see the opening event so successful. The grand march was led by Mr. Darling with Mrs. F.N. Davis, the president of the VIS.

Two VIS couples took charge of the dance each week, under a schedule that covered the whole season, June 1 to August 31. The VIS ran the dances twice a week. Those were the days of the real dance bands, and many different ones are noted in VIS records. People came many miles to enjoy dancing at the Boulders, including patrons from Lyndonville.

During its earlier years the casino earned a profit of $1,223.28 at the tearoom. One year the two enterprises netted the VIS $5,892. After 1926, when both facilities lost money, Mr. Darling recommended that the casino and the Boulders tearoom be leased to one person. When Mr. Darling died in 1931, the VIS involvement at Willoughby Lake ended and the Darling properties at the lake were sold to D.I. Grapes of Lyndonville and managed by his son Clarence.

Elmer Darling had designed a boat, the *Burklyn*, named for his mansion on the Burke-Lyndon town line near East Burke. This motor launch was built for him in Canton, Ohio, and shipped to a local station by rail and

The Boulders Tearoom.

The Boulders Dance Casino, deserted for years now, was built in 1921 by Elmer Darling for the benefit of Lyndonville VIS. Dancing took place upstairs and a restaurant was on the ground floor.

then drawn by horses to Willoughby Lake. This thirty-five-foot Mathews Day Cruiser was made of oak and mahogany, with brass fittings and cupboards with etched glass doors. It was one of the first motor launches on the lake. Clarence Grapes refitted the motor launch with a fine Chrysler marine engine and renamed it the *Mountain Maid*. Clarence operated it as a passenger boat for "the enjoyment of the public."

Some of us young people used to pile into a friend's car his father let him use and go to the Boulders a few times on a Tuesday evening. It was great fun dancing to the music of H. Guy Dunbar's Versatile Band in the upstairs dance hall. At that time we were usually dancing to Dunbar's Band every Friday night in Lyndonville. During intermission at the Boulders, we could promenade on the long upstairs roofed, but open, porch, where we could see the moon shining on the water of Willoughby Lake and enjoy a snack in the restaurant downstairs. We always had a lot of fun and after the dance we would drive back to Lyndonville happy to have been dancing at the Boulders. This, of course, was when Clarence Grapes was managing the Boulders.

Thus it was that for many years the public still had the enjoyment of the tearoom, the Boulders dance pavilion and even the motor launch. Though these were all being managed by Clarence Grapes after his father D.I. Grapes bought the properties in 1935, they all began with Elmer Darling and continued to be enjoyed many years after he died.

Elmer Builds His Dream House

Elmer could look out across the valley to Burke Mountain from his Mountain View home. The mountain was always a source of inspiration to all the family. When it seemed that a lumber company might "begin to ravage the slopes of the mountain and destroy its forests," Mabel Hall Walter wrote, "Elmer bought over 1000 acres of land there to preserve the beauty of the mountain."

While the Fifth Avenue Hotel was a big factor in bringing growth to that part of New York City, development began to surpass it and the fabulous hotel that had been considered too far uptown became too far out of town and was closed in 1908. Even before that, Elmer, sensing the inevitable, began to turn his thoughts more and more to his native Burke and his dream of building a mansion on the height of land near his Mountain View Farm.

Elmer's studies in architecture no doubt led him to dream about the great house of his own design that he would someday build in his native town in the sight of Burke Mountain. He also may have been inspired by his Uncle Alfred's beautiful estate, which he sometimes visited in New Jersey, just across the Hudson River from New York City. Elmer's dream became closer when he realized that the Fifth Avenue Hotel would be closed and demolished to make way for a new and immense business building. Elmer studied the lay of the land on the ridge in Burke where he wanted to build his new house. He drew plans for it and turned them over to Jardine, Kent and Jardine, Architects, at 1262 Broadway in New York.

Elmer got things underway in Burke, but his work was still at the Fifth Avenue Hotel for the time being. While the house was under construction starting in 1904, his brother Lucius was overseer of the work, managing details of supplies and labor. Mrs. Hall wrote, "Great slabs of granite were quarried on Kirby Mountain and teams with six and eight horses dragged the huge rocks down from the mountain, through the village of East Burke, and on up to the building site for the foundation." Most of the lumber for the house, an estimated 300,000 feet, was cut from Elmer's own forests and dressed in the mills at East Burke.

Elmer A. Darling.

Because of his experience in the Fifth Avenue Hotel, he knew where to get the people to make it the fine home he desired. Correspondence from Jardine, Kent and Jardine, Architects, and J.M. Foye, the carpenter and builder from St. Johnsbury, shows that the year 1904 was devoted to the basic structure of Elmer's new house. Heating, plumbing and flues were basic needs to begin his house. By December 29 of that year, a letter from Hoggson Brothers begins to talk of the decorations for the house with an estimate of $5,500. Elmer was dealing with New York companies, and he was no doubt familiar with the work they may have done at the Fifth Avenue Hotel.

Not particularly inspired by the "gilded opulence" of contemporary Victorian architecture, Elmer chose to go back into the past to a time when the country's great houses "were being erected in the stately sophisticated grandeur of the Georgian style," according to Allen Hodgdon of Lyndon State College in 1970.

The house was built three stories high with eight entrances. The main entrance is flanked by a two-story porch. Two side entrances open from the great hall, one toward the east with a large lawn and the other toward the west with a large sloping lawn. There are broad piazzas on three sides, which make a good place for exercise on stormy days, someone suggests, as fourteen trips around these piazzas will measure a mile. The steep roof is topped by a platform. From here one could admire the 360-degree view of

Burklyn Hall in the making. Elmer is on the roof, while the horse waits with the buggy.

the Green and White Mountains, the rolling pastures and the farms in the foreground.

There is very little ornamentation. Elmer chose to use ornamental details only on the doorways. Though sensible and serviceable, the interior was furnished in restrained elegance chosen for comfort as well as pleasing the eye. After all, one does not spend almost forty years in a hotel as elegant as the Fifth Avenue without an appreciation of beautiful appointments.

Elmer had designed Palladian windows, a hipped roof and a two-story portico front. On the floor of the portico is an embedded brass plate that indicates the four directions. Burke Mountain is in the southeasterly direction from the mansion.

The fourteen-foot great hall is paneled in painted white woodwork with mahogany pilasters. The fireplace is accented with two mahogany pilasters. The overmantel is dominated by the Darling coat of arms, with the motto, "Dei Donum" (Gift of God). Elmer followed the example of English Georgian homes with imported marble for mantel facings. The one in the hall is African marble. The staircase is a copy of the central stairway in Henry Wadsworth Longfellow's home in Cambridge, Massachusetts. It is appealing "with its hand-turned balusters—three to a step—with a walnut handrail. Forming a volute atop a spirally turned newel." Four large rooms are grouped around the main hall: drawing room, library, sitting room and

Entrance to Burklyn's north side portico.

dining room. In the south wing beyond are the kitchen, pantries, storeroom, a private dining room, a servants' dining room, conservatory and laundry. The main dining room is stately, with wainscoting around three sides and a mantel of mahogany carved in a "dignified but ornate character." It has a beamed ceiling with plastered panels. The color scheme is blue. A built-in niche is decorated at the top with a carved shell and cornucopia motif. The niche is lined with shelves for holding china and ornaments.

The sitting room gives an air of sociability with the masculine simplicity of its design in decorations and furnishings. The drawing room, which is also the music room, is done in the style of Louis IV, the walls paneled with rose-colored satin with corresponding draperies. "The ceiling is very elaborate with its ornamental plaster moldings forming a border around an oval center portion which has a painted design off clouds in light hues of blue, pink and white."

The library is equally beautiful and refined, with a more subdued and cozy feeling of colonial times. The overmantel is elaborately crowned with a well-designed scroll pediment, topped with a lamp symbolizing knowledge. The red Italian marble facing on the fireplace incorporates a clever design of an open book.

The private dining room, or breakfast room, in the south wing is flooded with light from a Palladian window. The town line goes directly through this room. It has been noted that when Elmer and his sister Louise sat down at the table, one was sitting in Lyndon and the other in Burke. No one has told me who sat in which town.

The dining room. The Amacita replica on the mantel is a wine cooler.

The sitting room.

The library.

The upstairs hall.

Louise's room, called Egypt because it looked toward the Little Egypt section of Lyndonville.

The four principal bedrooms were on the second floor, each with its own bath and ample closet space and each with a sterling nameplate on the door giving a name to each room. They were named for the direction they overlooked. The first letter of each name was worked into the painted design of the corner of each ceiling. The guest rooms were Brighton and Willoughby, because the rooms each looked toward those areas. Elmer's room was Franconia, looking toward that town in New Hampshire. Louise's room was Egypt, not because it faced Asia, but because it looked toward the district on the West Burke road in Lyndon that was called Little Egypt because it was a barren, sandy area. The south wings divide into seven smaller bedrooms, and the third floor contains several rooms for servants.

The central vacuum cleaner operates from the motor in the cellar and also there is a gas machine to use when the electricity is off. Elmer furnished one room to resemble an old-fashioned pub, complete with a brass rail from the Fifth Avenue Hotel. The wine cellar is secured with the original door from the hotel. I interviewed Lawrence Munkittrick years ago. He had been a butler at Burklyn Hall. He told me that when Elmer wanted wine for his dinners and parties, he would ask Lawrence to go down to the wine cellar with him, and then Elmer would unlock the door and tell Lawrence what he wanted brought out. The butler never had the key to the wine cellar in his possession.

Lawrence also told me that when someone came to the door Elmer would say, "Who is it, and what does he want?" When Lawrence told him who it was, Elmer would tell him to ask the visitor in and he would be very nice to whomever it was.

The billiard room, sometimes referred to as the clubroom, extends from the west end of the house. Between this and the main house is a covered driveway, or porte-cochere, where guests may arrive and enter either the mansion or the billiard room protected from elements, whatever the weather might be offering.

At the south end of the mansion is an extensive greenhouse and conservatory. A Dutch gardener, I believe his name was Nicholas VanTil, kept flowers blooming and ready for guests' bedrooms, as well as bouquets and arrangements for the main rooms downstairs. Earle Brown from Minnesota, a later owner who took very good care of the beautiful home, walled in the glass section to be used for an office. He sold off the Morgan horses and brought in Belgians. He brought a beautiful six-horse team hitched to a handsome wagon, which made a big hit in the cavalcade at the Caledonia County Fair in Lyndonville every year.

Elmer Furnishes His House

As there has been much written about Burklyn Hall itself, it seems readers might also be interested in the furnishings Elmer chose for his abode. He was able and willing to pay for quality to make a fine home where guests would be comfortable.

By June 1905, Hoggson Brothers, the contracting designers, had submitted specification furnishings for every room in the house. The first page of the specifications lists the furniture for the following rooms: entrance hall and main hall to be Italian oak; parlor to be Circassian walnut and gold; library, sitting room and dining room to be mahogany; room over parlor to be mahogany; room over library to be satinwood; and the room over sitting room to be Circassian walnut.

These specifications also list the furniture for every room, including such items as an umbrella jar for the entrance hall. For the music room, a grand piano and a music cabinet were included. Each room would be well and comfortably furnished, including settees, easy chairs, sofas, side chairs, a roll-top desk and a typewriter in the sitting room. The table in the dining room was a five-foot round extension table.

The specifications included the rugs for each room, many of them to be Oriental. For the sitting room it was a hand-tufted rug, and the four main rooms on the second floor were to be furnished with Wilton carpets. On July 1, 1905, Oriental rugs were ordered by Hoggson Brothers, namely Kermanshah for the drawing room; Indian punjab for the dining room; Indian pushmina for the library; Indian punjab for the sitting room; and Persian muskabed for the main hall and side hall. Also in July, Hoggson ordered andirons for Elmer—some brass, some gilt, for all ten fireplaces in the house. The cost was $1,540.

The following note from Jardine, Kent and Jardine is dated November 2, 1905: "Aug. 3, 1904—Design for granite watering trough to be erected at East Burke, no charge. Vt. Jan. 10, 1905, Instructions with sketch received from you for plans of a private stable to be erected at East Burke."

A letter to E.A. Darling, dated December 28, 1905, includes these words: "I received your very kind remembrance in the shape of the little calendar

Above: Burklyn Hall in all its glory.

Right: The Darling coat of arms.

which it is always a pleasure to have before me on my desk. I thank you very much for the kind thought. Wishing you an extremely happy New Year in which I hope complete satisfaction with the new house will figure, I remain, Yours very sincerely, W.W. Kent."

Elmer designed the furnishings, which were excellent pieces for a Victorian style, but as Allen Hodgdon wrote, they "detracted from the atmosphere created by the balance in the arrangement of the interior design." When the fourth owner of Burklyn Hall, C.H. Davis, sold the Vermont Tap & Die Company and holdings to the American Saw & Tool Company, many of the furnishings from Burklyn Hall went to Louisville, Kentucky.

Lighting fixtures listed for all the rooms in a Hoggson Brothers specification were electric, with gas tips for emergencies so they could convert to gas, which would come from the gas machine in the cellar. When the electric plant at the dam in East Burke closed at midnight, or for any other reason, the lights could be changed from electricity to gas. Sometimes when a party was going on, Elmer would telephone down to the plant and ask the operator to stay and keep the electricity on a little longer.

Hoggson Brothers got blueprints of elevations and the interior of the house from Jardine, Kent and Jardine so they could propose treatment for the main rooms. "The Curtains to be prepared with pulley cords to they can be drawn back, and when windows are open will not blow about." Furniture, bedding, slipcovers and cushions were all taken care of.

In 1906, a handsome safe came to Burklyn from the Mosler Safe Co. at 373–375 Broadway, New York. "One vault shipped to Lyndonville." The bill was settled with cash and eighty dollars were addressed to Elmer at the Fifth Avenue Hotel. When I was volunteering for Friends of Burklyn at Burklyn Hall, I remember the vault between the dining room and the breakfast room. The safe, a large one, is still at Burklyn Hall.

In June 1907, Elmer ordered dishes from the Gorham Co. of Fifth Avenue, such as tea sets, a water cooler, a chafing dish, pitchers, coffee sets and everything needed to serve his guests at dinner parties he intended to host in the manner he was accustomed to at the Fifth Avenue Hotel. In that year, Hoggson Brothers were putting the finishing touches on the rooms—upholstering, installing switch plates and chain pulls and placing furniture in position, including necessary touching up and rubbing to put the same in good condition.

A 1904 bill from Jardine, Kent and Jardine estimated the cost of the house to be $80,550.00. February 4, "Received payment, Jardine, Kent & Jardine." This was for $2,500 toward "numerous sets of prints, small and large scale and detail drawings of exterior and interior work, correspondence, &c. &c $4,027.50."

In 1909, there were still some furnishings specified, bedding, mats, small tables, cushions, etc. A July 15, 1909 invoice stated that eleven mezzotints were ordered from Hoggston. These were to be framed in black and gold molding. The prints were *Lord Nelson, David Garrick, Granville Earl Gower, John Lord Legionier, Sir William Chambers, Rev. William Paley, Mr. Tattersall*, another *David Garrick, Dr. Samuel Jonson, George Washington* and *Gov. Pownall*.

In 1910, Elmer received from Gorham Co. and paid for butter spreaders, a butter pick, a tea caddy, bottle holders, nameplates and twelve chocolate spoons. Then he ordered and paid for things like combs, hairbrushes, a buttonhook, a pin tray, a nail polisher, a powder puff, cologne bottles and the like.

Elmer had been described as dignified, reserved, shy, having a dry sense of humor and not loquacious, although he did like to tell stories. Elmer enjoyed parties and he liked to have everyone else enjoy them too. He always had special favors for all his guests and they all fit the occasion of the party—hatchets and bunches of ornamental cherries for a Washington's Birthday dinner, flags for Fourth of July, Easter eggs and so much more.

Elmer apparently enjoyed outings, as this clipping from the *Vermont Union* of August 4, 1909, says, "E.A. Darling and party of friends, Mrs. H.E. Folsom, Mr. And Mrs. John B. Chase, Miss Florence Chase, and George Chase, left last week Wednesday on automobile trip of five days stops being made at the Profile House, Mt. Washington House, (these two places in N.H.), Poland Springs Hotel in Maine; and the Waumbek, Jefferson, N.H. The party returned home Sunday afternoon."

Louise A. Darling, born October 30, 1854, was educated at LaSalle Seminary in Auburndale, Massachusetts. Not being in the best of health, she lived at home with her parents, Henry and Mehitable, and her brother Lucius also lived there until he married. It was also Elmer's residence when he was home from New York City. When the Mountain View Farmhouse, was renovated, they all moved up there from East Burke village. Elmer thought they would enjoy the more spacious house and the surroundings with Burke Mountain in full view. Louise stayed with her parents at their home, the Mountain View Farmhouse, and took care of them as long as they lived. When Burklyn Hall was completed in 1910, she moved there and became a most gracious and efficient hostess for her brother Elmer.

In the days when many people amused themselves by simply taking a Sunday afternoon drive not far from home, Mountain View Farm and Burklyn Hall were great attractions and lured Sunday drivers to Darling Hill for a leisurely hour or so. Not only was it a pleasant drive along the road, shaded on both sides by trees that formed a canopy overhead, but you could stare in awe at the great barns; the neat, well-kept houses; the

Louise Darling, sister to Elmer and Lucius.

Louise Darling became the hostess of Burklyn.

Haying the lawn at Burklyn.

great mansion, Burklyn Hall, standing handsomely on the rise above the sloping lawn; and the deer Mr. Darling kept pastured across the road from the mansion.

When I was a little girl, I remember taking those drives with my folks and my brother a few times. It was the first time we ever saw a peacock proudly spreading his beautiful tail as he strutted in front of one of the big barns. We usually saw the deer too. *The American Horse Breeder* of December 10, 1907, under "Mountain View Farm," tells much about the Morgans at the farm, but also says, "We must not forget the antlered buck, monarch of the little herd in Mr. Darling's private deer park."

Christmas at Darlings

After Elmer built Burklyn Hall, he liked to share his good fortune with the people of his native town and the area. He especially enjoyed staging Christmas parties for the children and grown-ups of East Burke. These were held in whatever building was newly constructed at Burklyn. For instance, some villagers remembered going to one in the creamery that was built to process the milk from a one-hundred-cow Jersey dairy into cheese and butter. The skimmed milk was fed to calves and pigs. One Christmas party was in the new garage across from Lucius's house, and one was in the Burke Mountain Club House in East Burke village.

John Chase, the *Vermont Union-Journal* editor, wrote of one Christmas party given on December 29, 1912:

> There were "high jinks" at the new barn last night when a Christmas tree party for the East Burke children was given by E.A. Darling. It was held in the new barn nearly completed with an interesting big clock with a fine toned bell. Gate posts of the large courtyard held big electric lights.
>
> It was a perfect winter night, everything mantled with snow, clear, bright stars overhead, and a big round moon rising above the dark border hills near Burke Mountain brought every curving hill top, every tree, and fence and smallest object into plain relief.

About 140 children and 50 or 60 grown people arrived about eight o'clock. They gathered in the big lobby of the barn, and the air was filled with the fragrance of new pine boards and a pleasant fire in the kitchen stove. While everybody waited for Santa Claus, an orchestra from Lyndonville furnished music and someone told a Christmas story. Santa Claus, though late, appeared in high good humor and led the children in a merry dance about the barn and then upstairs, where a wonderful Christmas tree "paralyzed the tongues of old and young." But Santa's tongue kept up with the nimbleness of his feet while he hurried here and there distributing presents. Everybody got a present and "we noticed in different cases how they happened to

Santa ready to come down the chimney at Burklyn.

The beautiful Christmas tree in the barn.

get 'just what I wanted'"—whether it was a doll, a handbag, a knife or a harmonica. Everyone received a silk flag, and the singing of the "The Star Spangled Banner" ended the program. But there was more.

Carrying their gifts, everyone returned to the lower floor where hot chocolate, ice cream and cake awaited them. The long barn was a fine place for marching, and the orchestra furnished good music for promenades. As everyone left for home, each child received a bag of candy.

Elmer kept lists of the children and what gift they had received each year, similar to Santa "making a list and checking it twice." He must have done or had someone do some detective work before the Christmas parties. At the 1926 party in the new Mountain View Farmhouse garage, one girl was heard to wish for a sled of her very own. Sure enough, there was a sled for her with her own name already on it.

Ida (Lang) Wheeler recalled in particular the Christmas party Elmer gave in the conservatory that he built on the south end of the mansion. Some people called it the "round room." "Mr. Darling would send sleighs or sleds to East Burke village to pick up the children who would gather at Harris's Store to wait for the big event," said Mrs. Wheeler.

The following is Mrs. Wheeler's account of that party.

The first Christmas party sponsored by the Darlings was held at the mansion. Fifty or more children sat on elevated seats inside the hothouse with a beautiful tree near the center. Ice cream and cookies were served, a rare treat in winter in those days.

Jolly old Santa then appeared, whom I learned later to be Fred Davis, caretaker of the Morgan horses. Following the singing of a few Christmas carols, Santa proceeded to present the lovely gifts. My name was called first. Being country shy, I was pushed onto my feet by children around me to receive a beautiful doll dressed in blue. It had been said that sometimes Elmer played Santa himself. The children were transported back to East Burke village on large sleds each drawn by a pair of Darling's beautiful horses.

Mrs. Wheeler reminisced much more about the Darlings and East Burke as it was in those days, and she never forgot the lovely doll she received in the conservatory Christmas party.

Linda (Smith) Gardner also recalled Christmas parties. One was in the fern room before the flowers were in there. Another was in the Morgan horse barn, one in the garage and one in the creamery. Gifts were sometimes clothing and toys, and popcorn and candy were served. "One gift I remember was cloth enough so my mother made me two dresses," Mrs. Gardner told me.

Morgan Horses at the Darling Farms

The Vermont Morgan horse breed was known all over the United States. "They were excellent for working, riding, pulling carriages or sleighs, and looking smart doing it too. They could outdraw, outrun, outwalk or out-trot any horse in the area. The rich, hilly pastures of Vermont gave them their great bone, muscle, wind and endurance," wrote Arthur Simpson in "The Morgan Horse," an article that appeared in the autumn 1955 issue of *Vermont Life*.

Elmer Darling was one local breeder of Morgan horses. The Darling horses and cattle from Mountain View Farm took many trophies at fairs and shows. Arthur Stone wrote in *The Vermont of Today*,

> *Here he started breeding Morgans, working with others in reviving interest in a passing breed. Mr. Darling has won at least a half dozen grand champion cups at the State Fair, and in past years exhibited Morgans at Madison Square Garden, where he carried off many a blue ribbon. Only one or two other Vermont breeders have so consistently exhibited the Morgans with continuous success and his handsome horses are always greatly admired at all the fall fairs.*

In 1908 the September *Vermonter*, the state fair issue, wrote, "The leader of the Vermont horses was Carrie, the trophy winner of 1907, a brown mare from E.A. Darling's Mountain View Farm at East Burke. She was a winner of many other prizes and was easily one of the most charming animals on the grounds." The class was for horses conforming most truly to the ancient Morgan type.

A group of men, mostly Vermonters, founded the Morgan Horse Club at the Vermont State Fair in White River Junction on September 23, 1909. Among its members were E.H. Hoffman of Lyndon, Allen Fletcher of Cavendish (who became governor of Vermont in 1912) and Elmer Darling of East Burke. The purpose of the club was "to perpetuate the Morgan breed of horses by preserving the original blood and type rather than by effort to

A fine pair of Morgans, with Fred Davis and Lucius Darling out for a drive.

H.R.C. Watson, C.C. Stillman, A. Phillips, E. Darling, H. Wardner and J.B. Estes. This photo was taken at White River Junction, State Fair, September 1915.

bring about improvement or change in size, speed or other features." The *Vermonter* once stated, "The membership of the club already includes every well-known breeder of Morgan horses east of the Mississippi river."

In the *Vermonter* magazine, the September 1909 issue reports, "The most striking horse among the twenty-five was the seal brown or dark bay four-year-old Bobby B., owned by E.A. Darling of East Burke." In the class for mares and geldings, "four-year old or over shown in harness," the winner was E.A. Darling's brown mare, Carrie, "good for first place in almost any class." "She has been a great winner at other Vermont State Fairs," said the *Vermonter*. A chief attraction at the fair was a class for horses "foaled outside Vermont." The winner was "the compact and sprightly Jennie C." driven by owner Joseph C. Brunk, who brought her to the fair from Rochester, Illinois. While at the fairgrounds, Mountain View Farm bought Jennie C. from Mr. Brunk and planned to keep her for breeding purposes. "Her short back, her short, flat but very nimble legs, her proudly carried head and neck are typically Morgan," said the *Vermonter*.

A report of the Caledonia County Fair, which was in St. Johnsbury from 1843 until it closed for good around 1930, said on September 24, 1919, "It will be a good long while before the race of Morgan horses is extinct. No one in these part is doing more to keep the strain strong and pure than E.A. Darling of Mountain View Farm, East Burke, who shows the string of prize winners which came from the state fair with so many ribbons." At the head of the string was Bob B. by Bob Morgan, who won in his class at the state fair. The twenty-four-year-old broodmare Hazel had a promising foal, Lyndon H. by Lyndon. Her five-year-old daughter Hazella by Lyndon was a perfect type of the old-fashioned chestnut Morgan. Little Justin, an eight-year-old gelding by Lyndon, was driven in a marched pair at the state fair and won the blue ribbon. Other entries of Darling's Morgans mentioned in the clipping are Woodbury, Don by Donald, Bob H. Jennie Woodbury by Ethan Woodbury, Jennie C., Lucy and foals by Sir Ethan. These are all familiar names to many of us who grew up in this area.

In researching the life of Elmer Darling several years ago, I called on Elmer's nephew, Henry Darling, at his home in Lyndonville. He told me how the horses were trained at Burklyn. He said the trainer would sometimes take the Morgans into deep snow so they would learn how to step high, wide and handsome. The horses learned not to shy or jump when somebody beside the road where they were walking or trotting made quick movements, such as suddenly opening an umbrella. The well-trained Morgans became good show horses and earned many trophies for the Darlings. Henry showed me the many horse and cattle trophies that were in his possession as the last close living member of this branch of the Darling family.

Bob B., winner of many trophies.

Elmer A. Darling of East Burke, president of the Morgan Horse Club, after a long connection in the Fifth Avenue Hotel in New York, came back to the place of his birth in 1907 and began his activities which have meant so much to Vermont. Burke has profited from his presence—and presents—marvelously although his benefactions extended far beyond the borders of that village.

The American Jersey Cattle Club

The American Jersey Cattle Club (AJCC), founded in 1868, held annual meetings in various places, but from 1885 until 1907 the club met at the Fifth Avenue Hotel. It probably would have continued to meet there if the hotel hadn't been closed and demolished in 1908.

Paran Stevens was a member of the American Jersey Cattle Club. The *Practical Dairyman* ("A practical weekly for dairymen and dairy stock interests") of April 9, 1908, when the Fifth Avenue Hotel was to be torn down, published an article with this heading: "The Famous Fifth Ave. Hotel, Its Owners, and Their Importance to Jersey History."

It tells the story of how Alfred B. Darling started his Jersey herd. "Paran Stevens was the owner of the Jersey cow Daisy. He was very proud of her but, even more proud of the exceedingly rich milk she gave and of the high color of it. At that time most milk made and sold in New York was from swill fed cows and of a very low order both in flavor and in quality."

The article goes on tell how every morning a glass of Daisy's milk was placed on Stevens's desk. He liked to leave it until the cream line became really noticeable. He was a person of a rather irascible temperament and the clerks knew his mood by the way he dealt with the glass of milk. If he was in a good temper, he would praise the virtues of Daisy, making sure to show the cream on top. If he was in a bad temper, he just gulped it down and said nothing.

To Alfred Darling, always full of life and fun, this was a source of great amusement. He delighted in teasing Mr. Stevens, telling him that someday he would own a cow who would give richer milk than Daisy. Mr. Stevens told him that he would never find such a cow. Mr. Darling took up the dare and imported Violet and Premium of Darlington from the Island of Jersey, for the sole purpose of possessing a better cow than his partner. This was 1869 and in this friendly spirit of rivalry the foundation of the Darlington herd was founded, soon to be known all over the world as one of the greatest Jersey herds of that time.

Elmer's Jerseys grazing in the sight of Burke Mountain.

Alfred Darling did not then own a farm, so the two Jersey cows were kept by a Mr. Smith on his farm in New Jersey. Mr. Smith was supplying the Fifth Avenue Hotel with dairy products from his farm at that time.

In 1872, Alfred Darling bought a valley farm in Ramsey, New Jersey, where he kept his "Darlington Herd." At a public sale on April 17, 1873, he bought eight more cattle from Richard Hoe of printing press fame: Eurotas 2454, a yearling; Leda 799; Rachel Ray 1754; the bull Sarpedon 930; Helene 170; Dido 1234; Oriole 2563; and the bull Inachus. He took them, along with Violet and Premium, to his new farm in Ramsey. Alfred became a member of the American Jersey Cattle Club in 1878. His partner in the Fifth Avenue Hotel, Hiram Hitchcock, also had a Jersey herd in Hanover, New Hampshire.

Elmer Darling, Alfred's nephew, was elected a member of the AJCC on April 27, 1892, and was named a director the same year. During this first year in the club, Elmer served on the executive committee for breed tests at Columbian Exposition that were conducted from May to October 1893. When he was elected president in 1894, it was said that "he has earned the promotion by the services that he had hitherto performed." He remained as president for twenty-one years. In 1894, the club registered 2,000 animals a year. At the end of his term in 1915, registration had grown to 33,000.

Elmer Darling when
he joined the AJCC,
1892.

By 1929, according to the *Jersey Bulletin* of April 22, 1931, the registration had reached 75,690. During Elmer's presidency, the club established the Register of Merit in 1903.

The club bought a house on West Seventeenth Street near Fifth Avenue in 1892 for use as a club office, but after eighteen years the growing business rendered it inadequate. In addition to other problems, the building was not fireproof and the club had a great quantity of irreplaceable records. In 1911, President Elmer Darling was authorized to find suitable ground for a new fireproof building. At his own risk, Elmer purchased two lots at West Twenty-third Street and made the down payment. This was readily accepted by the club and a new building was erected at a cost of $111,482.

At the annual meeting in 1901, the club asked Elmer Darling to appoint another committee, of which he would be *ex officio*, to prepare demonstrations of the value of the Jersey as a dairy animal at the Louisiana Purchase Exposition to be held in St. Louis in 1904.

Elmer took pride in making the annual meeting enjoyable to the members. For a good many years as president he had pieces of Limoges china made to order in France at his own expense. They were placed at each plate as souvenirs for the guests at the banquet the night before the annual meeting. Some of the pieces were decorated with a cow or the arms of the club, an intertwined AJCC. The hotel charged two dollars per plate, but the actual cost was more like ten dollars per plate; this was Elmer's annual treat for the club luncheon.

At the annual meeting of the AJCC in 1930, an oil painting of E.A. Darling was exhibited and the club approved the purchase by popular subscription. When acquired, it was hung in the club office. Cordial thanks were extended to all members of the club and others who by their subscription made it possible to commemorate a man "who faithfully served the club for so long a period." It was signed by the committee, consisting of Wilfred W. Fry, E.S. Brigham and R.M. Gow.

An article in the *Practical Dairyman* of April 9, 1908, spoke about the "struggles" to obtain a higher price for milk.

> *Struggles between milk producers and distributors over the question of price for milk are growing more common. In two centers in New York State, Auburn and Pulaski, a lively campaign is under way. April was set as a date for an advance in price by the producers and in both places the distributors have refused to pay the desired prices. The dairymen threatened to feed their skim milk to pigs and chickens and sell the cream or ship the whole milk far afield. In Auburn the distributors, mostly "small peddlers," threaten in retaliation to go out of such an unprofitable occupation altogether.*

Does this sound familiar in today's concept of producers and distributors? It looks as though this problem keeps arising every so often.

The Creamery at Mountain View Farm

The *Jersey Bulletin and Dairy World* of February 4, 1925, ran a lead article about Mountain View Farm cheese by George M. Rommel of New York. He wrote, "Fifty years ago a young Vermonter went down to the great city to try his mettle and find his fortune. He had learned the hard lessons of thrift and economy, sobriety, hard work and honesty, to which the Vermont hills subject their sons and daughters."

Rommel tells how the milk from Elmer Darling's Mountain View Farm herd went to the local creameries. The Fifth Avenue Hotel also used a great deal of this good Vermont cheese. At first the cheese at Darling's creamery was made for the family's own consumption. Later they made cheese for the hotel, "and the first thing we knew we were in the cheese business," Mr. Darling said. They were getting orders from people who had tasted their cheese. People sent money for what they thought the cheese would cost. They got the cheese by return mail and a refund for any overpayment as well.

"When we saw we had something good," said Mr. Darling, "we went to work in earnest, put up a first-class building especially to manufacture the product and let the business grow as fast as it would." The exclusive Chevy Chase Club of Washington served Darling cheese to the members and every week a shipment went to John D. Rockefeller.

Disaster struck in March of 1894 when Mr. Darling's herd of high-bred Jerseys and Devon cattle showed signs of tuberculosis. Professor Rich of the Vermont Agricultural College was summoned and tested the herd. Seventy-seven of the ninety-two cattle responded unfavorably and were slaughtered, involving a loss of over $3,000. Swine on the place were also found to be affected and had to be killed. The grave in which these cattle were buried measured 160 feet long, 4 feet wide and 6 feet deep. The herd was replaced by a few choice heifers from the Burnham farm in Connecticut, increased by a judicious selection from time to time of the best Vermont-raised stock. All were subjected to the tuberculosis test before purchasing. Soon the herd numbered eighty head of uniform excellence, all healthy, hardy cattle. But another disaster hit when the dairy barn burned and all the records of the herd were lost. The herdsman was the only man who could swear an oath to the breeding of each cow, but he died.

Even though he was president of the American Jersey Cattle Club, Elmer no longer kept registered cattle. He put honor first and let the registration go because the records were gone and there was no way to check up. He would not "be a party to pure bred livestock transaction about which there might be the slightest doubt." The heifers were raised until they had their first calves, and if they were promising they were put into the herd, replacing some older cows. Replaced cows might be sold to local buyers. The herd was producing milk that made the same good cheese, butter and cream.

"The Mountain View Farm at East Burke still continues to manufacture a superior quality of cheese and butter for a select trade," wrote Stone in *The Vermont of Today* in 1929. "The cheese is shipped to the Eastern states as far south as Florida. Four hundred and fifty cattle, principally Jerseys, furnish the milk and cream supply. The herd is free from tuberculosis and is a distinct credit to the commonwealth."

The creamery Elmer built was just beyond the main farmhouse. It was furnished with a ten-horsepower automatic engine with a thirteen-horsepower boiler for power and heat. The engine ran the cream separator, pump and a mill where the grain used on the farm was ground. This mill, with a capacity of twelve bushels per hour, was eventually replaced with a larger one of the

Some of the "works" at the creamery.

Milk pails stacked in the creamery.

same pattern, the Appleton, made at Geneva, Illinois. In the past the principal product of the farm was butter, about six hundred pounds per month being shipped to New York, but in 1896 a complete cheese-making outfit was added. Frank McDonald, who was employed on the place for seven years, was in charge of the cheese making and turned out seventy pounds per day in eight-, thirty- and fifty-pound cheeses. These were kept ripening from thirty to forty-five days and were then shipped to New York.

An extension to the creamery contained the repair shop, which was also the gathering place of the men employed on the farm. Here were carpenters' and plumbers' tools, while eight closets with tools for each man furnished no excuse for "losing the hammer." Each man was assigned a closet, given a key and was expected to place his tools there and lock them up when not in use. Mr. Darling employed an average of twelve men in the creamery, some of whom lived in the cottages and farmhouses.

In *Burke: More Than Just a Mountain*, Phyllis Burbank wrote that she talked with Murray B. Davis, who told her about working on the Darling farm. He said there were one hundred Jersey cows and four men to take care of them. Then about twenty-five men lived in the boardinghouse, the present-day Wildflower Inn and restaurant, and some men roomed over the creamery. Elmer would probably be pleased to see a barn at the former boardinghouse turned into a children's play area with many games, toys and lots of fun things to do. Also, one barn houses animals for children to pet and enjoy.

Laughter and Fun with
Elmer A. Darling

In the spirit of the occasion and the spirit of the times, it seems best here to quote John B. Chase himself from the *Union-Journal* to preserve the spirit in which it was written. It is another compliment to Elmer A. Darling from the people who appreciated all he did for others in his own quiet way. The clipping in my files was undated, but my guess is it would have been during the time when he did so much for the benefit of the Lyndonville Village Improvement Society with some of his property at Willoughby Lake. The people listed as giving the party were Lyndonville people and many, probably most, of them were working with the VIS.

'Twas the wont in ye good old days when ye winter time began to come, for the country folk to gather together in squads, and to make merry parties. Warm did glow the hearts when they did meet in various ways and for reasons numerous that were thot up by different ones in the community. 'Tis well, when frosty winter comes sweeping down from realms of the northward, covering our land with purest white, that we should crisp up our footsteps to keep pace with the Winter King and extract the glow of health from his pure fresh air by proper exercise and a merry time.

While the very winter it just beginning, in a spirit of true old fashioned kindliness, did several of Lyndonville's women plan for a merry time and the occasion was like this:

To the northward of Lyndonville lives a gentleman whose hospitality has been constantly extended for years to a large number of people in unstinted measure. He has installed himself very securely in the affections of his friends and it was the thot of some of these to arrange a dinner and a good time in small appreciation off his many favors. The event was compressed into only one short evening's hours yet was an expression of a desire to cover a period of many years of grateful appreciation.

Motors containing 46 people went to St. Johnsbury early last Friday evening where arrangements had been made by Mrs. Gray at the old Governor Fairbanks residence which is now occupied by the Maple Grove

Do we detect the twinkle in the eye of Elmer Darling here?

Candy co. The stately residence, with its spacious grounds, retains the atmosphere of the distinguished people who have always occupied it. Some of the guests present last Friday night returned to a time when they were there and used to look upon this as sacred ground. In those days they cautiously approached to glance over the fence.

It was very pleasant to find many of the original furnishings, attractive floor coverings, foreign paintings, statuary, the big oak side board with its

95

carved motto, the library full of books, and to walk about the spacious rooms, they being ideal for just such a party as this.

While in the olden days the guests would have arrived in sleighs, they came to this party in motors, arriving about six o'clock. They were informally received and secured their dinner partners by means of numbers. Those present were: Mr. and Mrs. G.M. Campbell, Dr. H. Monford Smith, Mrs. Ellie Clark, Mr. and Mrs. Homer Watson, Mrs. H.E. Folsom, Miss Ida Pearl, Mr. and Mrs. H.J. Hubbard, Mr. and Mrs. W.C. Connor, Mr. and Mrs. E.J. Blodgett, Mrs. G.P. Ide, Mrs. J.B. Chase, Mr. and Mrs. Charles L. Stuart, Mr. and Mrs. Sumner Stuart, Dr. and Mrs. F.H. Davis, Miss Nellie Davis, Miss Irene Stimson, Mr. and Mrs. H.F. Wood, Mr. and Mrs. Charles Hale, Mr. and Mrs. C.B. Dodge, Mr. and Mrs. Clause Watson, Prof. and Mrs. O.D. Mathewson, Mr. and Mrs. H.P. Silsby, Mr. and Mrs. P.R. Griswold, Mr. and Mrs. Leon Curtice, William Jeffers, Mrs. D.R. Brown, Mrs. John Ahern, Mrs. J.W. Copeland, Charles M. Darling, and the guest of honor, E.A. Darling of Burklyn Hall.

Dr. Smith, in his usual happy way, presided as master of ceremonies and ushered the guests about seven o'clock to the dining room, where one long table was arranged for all. The long room was festive with Christmas greens, sprays of which with the red poinsettias, were hung at all the windows and the table looked gay with red carnations and red candles. Mrs. D.R. Brown and Mrs. P.R. Griswold had arranged these decorations with charming affect. The banquet, prepared by Mrs. Gray and her daughter, Mrs. Powell, was a six course affair with everything served of the best quality. The menu included: fruit cocktail, clam bouillon, with cream and bread sticks, celery, olives, nuts, roast turkey with cranberry jelly, and vegetables, chicken jelly salad with rolls, frozen pudding, cakes, candy and coffee.

Little verse favors at each plate furnished amusement in reading while midway of the dinner, a surprise was announced when Dr. Smith said that the post man had just left a bag of mail with letters for all present. Each guest found upon opening his letter a toast to some other guest, written rhyme. These were all of a very witty character and caused roars of laughter. Mrs. P.R. Griswold and Mrs. E.J. Blodgett appeared to know a great deal about the verses. The last letter was read by Mrs. G.M. Campbell and was a clever toast to Mr. Darling. At the conclusion of her reading she presented Mr. Darling with a box containing a memento of the esteem in which he is held by his friends.

After the dinner all repaired to the library to register, while tables were prepared for those who cared to play whist and the evening was concluded with informal sociability.

Burke Mountain Clubhouse and Library

With his house finished, Elmer never lost interest in improving and building, using his architectural skills. One thing he very much wanted to do was build a community center in East Burke. He tried to buy a house in the village for it, but the property he had in mind was not for sale. He was somewhat disappointed but didn't give up. Then someone made the suggestion that the mill yard right in the center of the village could be cleaned and would provide an ideal site for his proposed center.

The mill yard in question was on the site of the hotel that at one time had housed the library that was started more than a century ago by the Ladies Library Association. This hotel had burned down many years before; the library was then housed in several places and had no permanent home. The mill yard site apparently appealed to Mr. Darling, for he designed a building and had some architects draw up the plans.

The handsome Colonial-style Burke Mountain Clubhouse, built in 1919, is situated in the village where Burke Mountain rises in the background. Opposite the clubhouse and across a bridge over the Passumpsic River two roads meet, one going straight up the hill to Mountain View Farm and the other leading to Burke Hollow.

The clubhouse grounds were landscaped to a gracefully sloping lawn and included a fine bandstand with excellent acoustics, also designed by Mr. Darling. There is a comfortable apartment in the building for a live-in caretaker.

Elmer provided rooms for a permanent library with brick fireplaces with imported andirons, wide window seats and paneling of brown ash carefully selected from trees on Burke Mountain, which Elmer and Lucius then owned. The rooms were furnished in unaffected good taste, with a library table also of brown ash and handsome Windsor-style chairs. Valuable art objects were placed around the rooms, along with plants in the sunny windows.

Before Elmer built the clubhouse with the library rooms, the Ladies Library Association maintained a library in many places around East Burke

The Burke Mountain Clubhouse and Library, built by Elmer Darling in 1919.

village. The ladies started the association when Mrs. H.M. Hall received a letter dated January 1872 from Mrs. Julia Paddock of St. Johnsbury offering them half of their three to four hundred books with this provision: "You will form yourselves into an Association similar to the one we have had, pledging yourselves to add books yearly." The other half of the books were offered to the town of Barnet under the same conditions. The St. Johnsbury ladies offered further assistance and bookcases. Because the St. Johnsbury Athenaeum had opened in November 1871, it is assumed that the ladies no longer felt a need to keep up a library.

On January 30, 1872, fifty ladies met in East Burke, drew up a constitution and bylaws and elected an executive committee, officers and a book committee. A library room was acquired. In April 1876, this entry appears in the Ladies Library report: "Met this time at the residence of Mrs. P.D. Bemis, the Librarian, on account of the hall's being destroyed by fire." Some of the East Burke residents remembered going to various places for books after the hotel burned. Whoever was librarian kept the books in her home. Though it was a Ladies Library Association in name, dues were also accepted by men so they too could borrow books.

When Elmer built the Burke Mountain Clubhouse, the library finally had a permanent home. The Ladies Library Association maintained the library rooms and socials were held to raise money. In January 1920, the secretary reported, "Mr. E.A. Darling provided moving picture entertainment." Admission was ten cents. This serial viewing continued until the complete story of *The Count of Monte Cristo* was shown. Lucius's wife Margaret was a very active and helpful member of the Library Association and was its president for several years. She often provided refreshments and cakes made by her chefs at Mountain View Farm. Elmer's gifts included many books on Lincoln, a bust of Lincoln and tablets inscribed with the Gettysburg Address and the Emancipation Proclamation.

In 1874 the constitution and bylaws of the Ladies Library Association were printed in a booklet along with the library's first published catalogue of books. The list then contained 340 titles. One of the books on that list is still in the library today. It is the *Comic History of the United States* by John D. Sherwood. The book is full of comic sketches by Harry Scratchley. Students of United States history should read this jolly chronicle. Mr Sherwood wrote that the "tobacco was first grown in Virginia in 1616…although much piped about ever since has never ceased to create a smoke." He also reported, "Both New York and New Hampshire pouted and grumbled at the appearance of the newcomer [Vermont] and threatened to smother her in her cradle." He said, "Georgia was eyed by Oglethorpe although his intentions were honorable."

The ladies of 1872 would probably be delighted with the beauty of the library rooms and the number of volumes they contain today. Included are a great number of books from Elmer Darling's personal library. These contain bookplates imprinted with his name, which distinguishes them from the other books in the library. Titles include *The Harvard Classics*, *The Waverly Novels*, works of Dickens, Vermont books, humorous books, reference works, modern novels and also a number of valuable first editions. One particularly old book has been identified as a Bay Psalm Book. Elmer's books are all displayed in the south end room.

The library is now called the East Burke Community Library. The Burke Mountain Club and the library are separate organizations, both very much alive and active. The Burke Mountain Club meets each month. Some of its activities include programs with speakers, and sometimes suppers are held downstairs, where there is a kitchenette, dining room and another meeting room. A pool table is another added attraction, along with a supply of card tables. For several years when we lived in Mount Hunger in the town of Lyndon, but not far from East Burke, my husband and I went to weekly whist parties at the Burke Mountain Clubhouse.

Lyndon Institute

On a wall near the main entrance of Lyndon Institute, Inc., at Lyndon Center is a bronze tablet with this inscription: "Per Aspera Ad Astra" (Through hope to the stars). Lyndon Institute honors four men in grateful remembrance—Sumner Shaw Thompson, Dudley Pettigill Hall, Theodore Newton Vail and Elmer Albert Darling. Beneath Elmer's name it reads, "Sincere friend and generous contributor." Lyndon Institute, chartered in 1867 as the Lyndon Literary and Biblical Institution and changed in 1921 to Lyndon Institute, Inc., serves Lyndon and the surrounding towns as a fine independent high school. For many years Elmer Darling was a trustee of Lyndon Institute and a longtime president of the board.

When the main building, the handsome brick Thompson Hall, was completely destroyed by fire on the cold, windy night of January 2, 1922, the trustees immediately met and voted to rebuild. The trustees who were present pledged $30,000. The building committee consisted of Elmer A. Darling, Harley E. Folsom, W.W. Hubbard, Ozias D. Mathewson and John L. Norris. Mathewson was the headmaster of the school (a position that was called principal in those days).

Over six hundred individuals in Lyndon and the surrounding towns subscribed to the fund. The sending towns, which voted each year at their respective town meetings to designate Lyndon Institute as their high school, included Burke, East Haven, Newark, Sheffield, Sutton and Wheelock. The building was dedicated on December 21, 1922, with President of the Board Elmer A. Darling as master of ceremonies. The speaker was the former governor of Massachusetts, the Honorable Samuel Walker McCall, whose wife Ella Esther was the daughter of Sumner Shaw Thompson of Lyndon Center. She was a graduate of Lyndon Institute, class of 1874.

The building was ready for classes, which had met anywhere they could during the spring and fall semesters. Instruction had been moved to the building by the winter term in January 1923. Elmer Darling had a hand in designing the new edifice, a classical-style beautiful brick building with white columns and a belfry. It is thought, though unknown, that Elmer personally

Lyndon Institute's new main building after Thompson Hall burned in 1922. Elmer Darling, president of the trustees, helped to create new building and dedicated it in 1922.

contributed a large amount of money so the building could be constructed quickly, but still with the best-quality work.

The class of 1926 dedicated the yearbook, *The Cynosure*, "To Elmer A. Darling, who as President of the Institute Board of Trustees, was largely responsible for the erection of the new building, and who, as friend, has contributed a great deal to the needs of the Institute. We, the Class of 1926 gratefully dedicate this third volume of the CYNOSURE."

Elmer's Surprise Eightieth Birthday Party

"**B**urklyn Hall Invaded By Host Of Friends on Saturday Evening" read an article in John Chase's *Vermont Union-Journal* in April 1928. "Not so much to remind him of his 80th birthday, as to show the warm affection in which he is held in the community, about 150 members of the Burke Mountain Club went in a body Saturday evening to Burklyn Hall and presented their most sincere felicitations and wished Elmer A. Darling many happy returns of the day."

The occasion was planned as a surprise by a committee from the club. Mr. Darling was completely unaware of the event, "but he was quick to recover his accustomed poise and promptly welcomed the neighbors and friends, mostly from Burke and Lyndon, to his commodious home." The "invaders" met at the home of Lucius Darling and "proceeded up the hill and so well was the event planned that the fortress was surrendered without a struggle and the owner was quick to capitulate."

The program was informal, with music consisting of a song by Miss Ruth Farmer with piano accompaniment by Mrs. B.W. Streeter. Mrs. Streeter also rendered a song and piano selection of her own. On behalf of the East Burke members, Reverend Lawrence Larrowe, pastor of the Federated Church, presented Mr. Darling with a beautiful motto, "House of Friendship," and three more appropriate words could not be selected in describing Burklyn Hall. The Lyndonville members, with Ozias D. Mathewson, principal of Lyndon Institute, as spokesman, presented Mr. Darling with carnations and two handsome books. Mr. Darling responded with heartfelt affection for East Burke, its past history and its present interests and people.

Editor Chase wrote,

> *Mr. Darling is a member of the Union League of New York, a trustee of the Polyclinic Medical School and Hospital of New York; has been president of the Jersey Cattle Club and of the Morgan Horse Club; was one of Vermont's delegates in the last Republican National Convention; is the president of the board of trustees of Lyndon Institute and a member*

of the board of trustees of St. Johnsbury Academy; is a director of the Lyndonville Savings Bank and Trust Company; is actively identified with recent building operations at Lyndonville, including the new Darling Inn, of which corporation he is president; as well as many other business and industrial railroad and manufacturing enterprises, here and elsewhere.

But it was not because of these important activities that his friends and neighbors called on him. Rather, his birthday was an excuse to extend cordial congratulations and expressions of appreciation "to a man who has done so much in his quiet, unpretentious way to the lasting benefits of the community in which he lives."

Darling Inn—The Gem in the Green

The fire that devastated a large portion of the Lyndonville business district on January 22, 1924, included the hotel then called Lyndon Hotel, formerly Webb's Hotel. The need for a replacement was still prevalent in those days and a group of subscribers was formed to build a new hotel. Directors of the group were E.A. Darling, O.D. Mathewson, H.E. Folsom, John L. Norris, D.I. Grapes and W.E. Riley, all prominent Lyndonville businessmen. Subscriptions were collected until 1927, when the group decided they could begin building.

Elmer A. Darling was chosen to head the enterprise. His long experience at the Fifth Avenue Hotel in New York City enabled him to contribute his finesse and expertise to the appointments of one of the finest hotels in the Northeast. He had a fine taste for fitness and proportion. He made sure only the best materials were used in the construction, from "the first stone in the foundation to the last cup in the kitchen." He requested and was given the privilege of personally furnishing the dining room.

The new hotel was named for Darling, though not at his request. His friends thought it a fitting gesture since he was a principal sponsor. When the hotel was dedicated in June 1928, Mr. Darling was eighty years old.

A big quarter-page ad in the *Caledonian-Record* of June 5, 1928, read, "Darling Inn, 'A Gem in the Green,' Lyndonville, Vermont. Official Opening, Thursday, June 7, A thoroughly modern hotel in every respect—Open the year 'round, European Plan, Rates $2.50 to $7.00." The catchphrase used for the hotel, "A Gem in the Green," was later adopted by the Lyndonville Board of Trade for promoting Lyndonville, and later became a slogan for the whole town of Lyndon.

The tall, arched windows with small panes at the Darling Inn gave the inn a colonial air and an abundance of light. Almost all guest rooms had private baths and all had telephones. The kitchen was electrically operated, even to a potato peeler. Cooking was done on a huge coal range and charcoal broiler.

In those days when the inn opened, the nearer portion to the handsome lobby was for gentlemen guests and the larger west end for the ladies.

The Darling Inn. Elmer Darling designed this handsome, lively hotel and helped build it. It is now senior apartments and the senior meal site.

Hardwood floors, plush rugs, Windsor chairs, a large fireplace and luxurious divans were the latest appointments for the ladies' comfort, while the men's section was furnished with both red and green leather chairs and mahogany tables. There was a cocktail lounge in the basement.

A smaller ladies' parlor was elegantly furnished, as was the Rotary Club room, where the Lyndonville Rotary Club held weekly meetings and luncheons. There was a piano in this room, a table, Windsor chairs, a desk, luxurious carpet and opalescent drapes shot with gold.

The Darling Inn was operated by the Lyndonville Hotel Company, and after a series of subsequent owners, Mr. and Mrs. Andrew Janis opened it as the Darling Inn Convalescent Home on January 14, 1964. It closed in 1978 and the Community Investment Company acquired the hotel and renovated it into twenty-seven units for senior citizens, opening as the Darling Inn Apartments. It is also the Senior Meal Site, serving full meals at noon, five days a week, except holidays.

The furniture in the dining room, chosen by Elmer Darling, is still in place, as are many of the dishes, and the Darling coat of arms still hangs over the fireplace.

From a scrapbook given to the Lyndon Historical Society by Lester and Marcelena Smith through Lori Charron Smith, July 1991, an undated

Alfred Darling greets Santa at the Darling Inn, circa 1950s. *Courtesy Beatrice Darling Ransom, Alfred's sister, who said, "Sorry the horse is not a Morgan."*

clipping says, "The Georgian type Darling Inn owned for the past three years by Mr. and Mrs. C.H. Davis was purchased this week-end by Sgt. Alfred H. Darling of Lyndonville, instructor at West Point. Darling expects to be able to devote his full time to operating the Inn about the first of the year." Alfred H. Darling was the son of Charles Melvin Darling, who was the cousin of Elmer.

Beatrice Darling Ransom, Alfred's sister, wrote me on March 11, 1978, that she remembered when Alfred and Helen owned the inn. They had a Christmas gathering for young and old and Santa came by sleigh. Children usually put on a little Christmas entertainment, and then there was singing of Christmas carols by all. The evening ended with refreshments.

About Twenty Thousand Visitors a Year Visit Darling State Forest Park

The following is adapted from the *Burlington Free Press*, July 14, 1962, by Harriet F. Fisher

East Burke—From the windswept rocky ledges on top of Burke Mountain, panoramic views spread out in every direction. Marked trails give people the advantage of views from several different points. Children love to crawl in the den-like places made by huge splits in the ledges. The summit rising 3,267 feet above sea level may be reached by automobile or, as some prefer, hiking by trail or road.

In 1933, Lucius and his son Henry G. Darling gave this land to the state, and with additional land, Darling State Forest Park now contains about 1,726 acres. When it was established as a state park in 1933, a Civilian Conservation Corps (CCC) encampment was set up at the base of the mountain.

These men developed the park by clearing out dead trees, building a road (later paved by the state) ending with a parking area near the summit and laying out a picnic area at the halfway point with a covered shelter, fireplaces and tables. They built a wooden fire tower to replace the one that had collapsed; this new tower met an end when the hurricane blew it down in September [1962]. The state replaced this one with a steel tower.

When the CCC left, they took down their buildings, which the state did not need. Only the remains of a large stone fireplace that was in the recreation hall was left of the CCC buildings. The corps also built the house at the park entrance. Made of fieldstone, topped by a second story of logs, it is ideally suited to the surrounding green forest. It fits in equally as well with the fall colors or the winter snow. Park custodian Carlos Powell, his wife and two children lived comfortably on the second floor. Mr. Powell said nearly two thousand visitors enter the Darling State Forest Park each year, the number being about equally divided between summer and winter.

The first-floor hallway, office and large meeting room are paneled in knotty pine. These rooms contain a big pine table with matching chairs, piano, stone fireplace and six large windows. The meeting room with

Darling State Forest Park building.

kitchen privileges may be rented for meetings or parties. Here also is the attractive showcase that displays the valuable collection of bells, including the thirteenth-century Korean temple bell.

Hanging in the trees a short distance away from the house are bells of even greater value—not because of material or antiquity, but because of their significance. These are wind bells—the Bells for Peace. The state of Vermont set aside two acres for the Bell Gardens. Other states and countries have contributed bells, either for the bell museum or wind bells for the garden, desiring to be represented in prayers for world peace.

At the interfaith service at the Bells for Peace Garden on Burke Mountain on Sunday [July 15, 1962], Perry Merrill, head of the state Department of Parks and Forests, stated that 1933 was a memorable year for him, as that was when Lucius and Henry Darling gave Burke Mountain to the state of Vermont for recreational use.

Governor Robert Stafford said that there is no more beautiful setting in the world than this one on Burke Mountain: "It is God's Cathedral." How lucky all of us are to live in a land with so much natural beauty. Governor Stafford declared that Burke Mountain "has now become a national shrine." The Bells for Peace Garden stood for the hope of peace throughout the world. However, because weather and high winds could cause damage to the bells, they were all placed in the bell museum.

Ski Burke, Inc., leases part of the park. A large parking lot, warming hut, Poma lift, ski trails, first aid patrol, ski instructors and a place for refreshments make this a mecca for skiers. Not far away in East Burke village are lodges and guest homes providing places for those who wish to spend weekends or whole vacations of skiing.

People who enjoy camping out in the summer are given ample opportunity and facilities at low fees. As one Vermonter said, "The best vacation we ever had was the time my wife and I took our children on a two-week vacation in state parks." A choice of camp sites provide at least nineteen tent platforms, three trailer sides and ten lean-tos throughout the park. All campsites have fireplaces, wood supplies and tables. Water taps and restroom facilities are nearby.

A forest fire watchman from the State Forest Service guards the entire surrounding area from the top of the fire tower on the highest peak. If a fire occurs, he has all the equipment necessary to determine the exact location and summon firefighters quickly to the scene. His home for the summer is a little cottage sheltered in the mountainside just below the peak.

The Lincoln Document

A small piece of paper with the famous signature, A. Lincoln, beautifully framed, was for many years owned by a family with their roots planted deep in Burke. The story of the Lincoln document goes back to a situation of the Civil War. Captain David Farragut won the Battle of Mobile Bay on August 5, 1864. Northern troops blockaded Mobile, Alabama's only port city. General Lee surrendered to General Grant on April 9, 1865. News was slow to reach the South (it was May before Confederate troops in Alabama and Mississippi surrendered).

This was the situation when Alfred B. Darling was wondering how things had fared in the Confederate city and decided to visit his property there (he had been a partner in the Battle House at Mobile since 1852). It would be natural for Alfred Darling to stop at the White House, since he was known to have some political clout. This enabled him to secure a personal pass from President Abraham Lincoln that would allow the bearer to pass through Northern lines.

The paper he secured read, "Allow the Bearer, A.B. Darling, to pass to and visit Mobile, if and when that city shall be in our possession. A. Lincoln, April 13, 1865." That date would be the last full day of President Lincoln's life, as he was assassinated the next evening, April 14. These facts, as well as the famous signature, transformed this pass into a treasured document in the Darling family.

Elmer inherited the pass from his Uncle Alfred. After Elmer's death in 1931 at Burklyn Hall, the certificate went to his brother Lucius. When Lucius died in 1937, ownership of the document passed on to his son, Henry G. Darling of Lyndonville. Henry died in 1986, and since he had no children, his wife, Kathleen Chaffee Darling, donated this valuable document to the Vermont Historical Society, where it could be displayed. The *Vermont History Newsletter* of March–April 1987 said, "The Vermont Historical Society is pleased and proud to be the inheritor of this very special Darling family treasure."

In addition, Kathleen also donated land to the village of East Burke across the road from Woodmont Cemetery to be used for recreational

Lucius A. Darling holds the family treasure, the Lincoln document.

purposes and to be named Henry G. Darling Recreation Park. The land had been owned by Henry's great uncle, Alfred B. Darling. In recognition of the family's monetary donations to Lyndon Institute over the years, the land around the main building was named the Darling Campus.

The Young Ladies Club

In 1925, Lucius started a memorial for his mother, Mehitable (Whitcomb) Darling. Women of East Burke who were sixty-five and older were invited to form the Young Ladies Club. Lucius remembered how much his mother had enjoyed many pleasant social affairs at the church, so he deposited some money into a fund to defray the expense of an annual banquet. The first banquet was held July 13, 1926. Seven of the twenty-three attending were over eighty years "young."

A dinner was held for many years, but eventually there was only enough money to have one every two years. Then one was held only every third year. Lucius would have felt bad to realize that the money he had provided for the ladies' enjoyment of a banquet once a year would have so little value in years to come due to inflation.

The Young Ladies Club had a memorial dinner at the church vestry on July 26, 1989, but the newspaper reported it as the "Young Woman's Club," to be politically correct I presume. Thirty-six people attended, with Phyllis Burbank giving a talk on the historic events of the Darlings. A movie was shown, depicting a group of working men in the village sitting and conversing by the old-fashioned stove in the Webster Store, now Bailey's at Burke. At a short business meeting, Blanche Gorham read the original minutes of the gift by Lucius A. Darling to the "young" women of Burke.

Many of these ladies also belonged to the Willing Workers, a church group that largely did work sewing for needy people. In an undated clipping, probably from 1928 or '29, seventeen ladies attended the regular meeting this group at the Burke Mountain Clubhouse. Late in the afternoon the "setting of stitches" was interrupted by sounds of a march and the ladies descended to the parlor, headed by Mrs. L.A. Darling, who was completely surprised at the sight of a pink-and-white birthday cake made in her honor by Miss Alice Bancroft. The pastor's wife, Mrs. Larrowe, voiced the general feeling of love and friendship for Mrs. Darling, and on behalf of the society presented her with a framed motto on friendship, a bowl of pink flowers and numerous cards from absent members. There were greetings from Mrs.

Carl Frasier, president of the Willing Workers, who was wintering in Florida. Mrs. Darling expressed her surprise and gratitude in a very feeling way. Mrs. Kelly served afternoon tea and Mrs. Darling cut the birthday cake.

The Young Ladies Club is still alive, but because the money Lucius funded for it does not stand up to today's inflation, the women meet for a banquet, lunch or dinner about once every two or three years.

Elmer A. Darling Dies at Burklyn

The *Vermont Union-Journal* of Wednesday, April 15, 1931, reported,

The death of Elmer Darling at his home, Burklyn Hall in East Burke, Saturday afternoon at 4:40 o'clock has brought to his native town of Burke, to all this section and the state of Vermont, an irreparable loss. So active and helpful has he been, for so many years, in all local affairs that his death brings to the people of his home town, to all who knew him, because personal contact with him inspired a friendly, trustful feeling to be greatly valued.

The funeral is held from the late home at 2 o'clock this Wednesday afternoon with burial in the family lot at Woodmont Cemetery, the officiating clergyman being Rev. Lawrence Larrowe of East Burke.

He had been in failing health for a year or so and confined to his bed for several weeks. His last ride to Lyndonville had been about ten weeks ago. The end came in his sleep and his eighty-third birthday would have occurred on April 22nd.

Mr. Darling's business activities were many and varied. He was always in close touch with all operations at Mountain View Farm. He was president of Lyndon Institute, one of the trustees of St. Johnsbury Academy, a director of the Connecticut and Passumpsic Rivers Railroad and president of the Lake Mitchell Trout Club.

He was especially prominent in promoting new buildings at Lyndonville after the disastrous fire that destroyed so much of Depot Street, as director in building of the new hotel, the Darling Inn, the Lyndonville Realty Company and other local organizations. He was a member of the Union League Club of New York City, the New England Society of New York, and many Vermont organizations.

He was a republican, and though not seeking office, was a delegate to the Republican National Convention in Cleveland in 1924. He was a director of the Lyndonville Savings Bank and Trust Co., and of the Lyndon Club, and of the Lyndonville Board of Trade.

Elmer designed this Corinthian-style tomb at the entrance to Woodmont Cemetery in East Burke.

There was a cordial welcome in his home that made his guests happy to be there, whether a few friends for dinner, or a large gathering for a moonlight party, a formal party, or an informal party.

Genial, friendly, modest, unassuming, was this personality, but now gone, and the sweet memory it leaves will not perish so long as there any here who have come in contact with him.

Elmer A. Darling Leaves Great Legacy

The front page of the *Caledonian-Record* of April 16, 1931, reported,

> *Public Bequests In* [Elmer] *Darling Will: Burke Mountain Club, $30,000; Congregational Society, East Burke, $15,000; Woodmont Cemetery, East Burke, $15,000; Lyndon Institute, $100,000; St. Johnsbury Academy, $10,000; University of Vermont, $5,000; Middlebury College, $5,000; Bennington College for Girls, $5,000; Town of Burke for Needy Account, $10,000; Burke Meeting House, $6,000; Brightlook Hospital, $10,000.*

A portion of the money that was left to Lyndon Institute ($50,000) was in memory of his sister, Louise A. Darling, to be known as the Louise A. Darling Fund. The other $50,000 was in memory of their brother, Scott E. Darling. These funds were to be used for general purposes.

The executors for the estate were his brother, Lucius A. Darling; his nephew, Lucius's son, Henry G. Darling; and Lyndonville Savings Bank and Trust Company. No public announcement was made of the extent of the Darling fortune and the many private and personal bequests.

The *Caledonian* had this to say about Elmer A. Darling:

> *Remarkably successful life ends after 83 years active years. The State of Vermont and his native town of Burke and this immediate vicinity in particular, suffers an irreparable loss. He would have been 83 years old if he had lived until April 22.*
>
> *He had been in failing health for many months and his death was not unexpected, but it, nevertheless, came with a deep sense of personal loss to everyone who knew him and had come to recognize his fine traits of character and his true philanthropic interest and real, personal concern in the well being of the community and state of which he was a part.*

For the last twenty years or so of his life, Elmer had divided his time between his real estate interests in New York and his Mountain View Farm, "an immense tract of land surrounding the home of his ancestors." Mr. Darling's life work was with the Fifth Avenue Hotel in New York City, but he always kept close touch with all the operations at Mountain View Farm.

He was president of the American Jersey Cattle Club for twenty-one years and had been president of the Morgan Horse Club, president of Lyndon Institute trustees, a trustee of St. Johnsbury Academy, director of the Connecticut and Passumpsic Rivers Railroad and president of the Lake Mitchell Trout Club. He was especially prominent in promoting the new buildings in Lyndonville after the 1924 fire, such as the Darling Inn, the Community Building and the Realty Block. He was a member of the League Club in New York City, the New England Society of New York and many Vermont organizations. He was Republican in politics; he never sought an office but was a delegate to the Republican National Convention at Cleveland in 1924.

Funeral services for Elmer A. Darling were at his home, Burklyn Hall, Wednesday afternoon, April 15, 1931, conducted by Reverend Lawrence Larrowe of East Burke. The bearers were O.D. Mathewson, W.E. Riley, John B. Chase, H.D. Webster, Frank Stoddard and Fay D. Warner. The burial was in Woodmont Cemetery at East Burke. Business was generally suspended in East Burke and Lyndonville and shades were drawn at St. Johnsbury during the services. Among those attending the services was Charles N. Vilas, who was with the Fifth Avenue Hotel for many years and was one of the last of the partners with Elmer Darling. He died in September 1931 at his Alstead, New Hampshire home.

Tribute to Elmer Darling

Mr. Ozias D. Mathewson was a graduate of Lyndon Institute in 1886 and helped form the permanent organization of Lyndon graduates in 1888 that became the Lyndon Institute Alumni Association, a strong and active organization to this day. He graduated from Dartmouth College Phi Beta Kappa in 1890. After twenty-two years as principal and superintendent of the Barre (Vermont) School System, O.D. Mathewson was hired in 1912 by Theodore N. Vail, then president of the institute trustees, to become principal of Lyndon Institute.

During his thirty-one years there, Mr. Mathewson was strong on discipline, but always fair. He taught many classes and was public spirited, serving the community in many ways. His high educational standards and long service earned him the reputation of being one of Vermont's outstanding educators. I personally am proud to be a graduate of Lyndon Institute, class of 1937.

Elmer Darling was a trustee and president of Lyndon Institute for many of the years that O.D. Mathewson was principal there. No better tribute to Elmer A. Darling exists than the following letter, written by a man "of the old school" himself, and signed by his distinctive signature.

April 17, 1931
Lucius A. Darling
East Burke, Vermont

Dear Mr. Darling:

I am taking this opportunity to write you a note expressing the appreciation of Lyndon Institute and its friends for your brother's magnificent bequest announced in the papers last night. I had known for some time of his intention to make such a bequest and had tried to express to him my deep appreciation of his generosity.

As you know, we were most intimately associated in various business enterprises for several years. Mr. Darling was a delightful man to be

Elmer Albert Darling.

associated with in any undertaking. He was quiet, unassuming, kind hearted, and considerate of the views and opinions of other people. We sometimes describe a person as "A gentleman of the old school." I never knew a man to whom the expression applied better than to Elmer A. Darling.

It is a source of satisfaction to me personally that affairs of the Institute have been so administered as to have won his approval and confidence so that he was willing to contribute so generously to the financial needs of the Institute.

May I express to you, Mr. Darling, and through you to the other members of the family, my deepest sympathy.
Yours sincerely,

[signed O.D. Mathewson]

As the Burke bicentennial papers have stated, "Enduring Burke Mountain stands tall above the resting places of those men and women who gave so much to this town. From the ski trails on the wooded slopes in winter, and the campsites in summer, echo the sounds of the laughter and joy in the beauty of the day…a fitting expression of thanks to those (and that includes the Darlings) who first came as pioneers to Burke."

Afterword

Burklyn Hall Property Sold

Burklyn Hall did not stand idle for long. It went through several owners after Elmer died. When C.H. Davis brought the Vermont Tap & Die, a tool company, to Lyndonville in 1933 it was a great boost for the area at a time when the railroad business was going down and the Depression in full swing. The Tap & Die gave employment to many. In 1948, Davis bought the Darling mansion, Burklyn Hall, eighty-six acres and a few nearby buildings that went with it from Earle Brown, who had decided to return to Minnesota. Davis also owned the Darling Inn in Lyndonville for a while. Then in 1957, Davis, ready to retire, sold the tool business and Burklyn Hall property to the American Saw and Tool Company for $1,500,000. This may be the time that Alfred M. Darling acquired the Darling Inn.

The *Caledonian-Record* of Saturday, August 31, 1957, reported, "Notable Gift to State—Burklyn Hall. It is a rare event when a large corporation newly arrived in Vermont is prompted to make a gift to the state of a property so valuable as the Burklyn farm home. Mr. Lee Thomas and the American Saw and Tool Company of which the Vermont Tap and Die Corporation is now a division deserve the admiration of all Vermonters." Instead of placing it on the market, "they are helping to further tangibly the cause of higher education in northern Vermont."

The offer was made several months before, and mention was made that it could be possibly used as a college, although the agreement signed on August 30, 1957, stated only that the property was to be used "exclusively for public purposes." The mansion was put to use as a men's dormitory for Lyndon State College in nearby Lyndon Center until more dormitories could be built on campus. LSC did get more dormitories and gave up the use of Burklyn Manor, as they had called it.

Friends of Burklyn

In 1970, Elizabeth (Shahler) Brouha of Sutton founded Friends of Burklyn with hopes of raising enough money to save the deteriorating Burklyn Hall and turn it into an arts center. Elizabeth was born in London and was raised in Belgium by American parents from Kansas. Her father was a geologist and mining engineer. Elizabeth was exposed to art during all of her twelve years of schooling in Brussels. Art classes were held in the museum and students had the run of the museum and got a feeling of art of the world. She learned the practicalities of life as well as art, including spinning and weaving wool from the sheep in their country place in Belgium. She saw America for the first time at age seventeen, when her father brought her to visit her grandparents.

When she was twenty-one she came to America and attended the Museum School of Art in Boston. Also in Boston was Lucien Brouha, whom she had met in Belgium. They were married in Belgium in 1938. In 1940 they came to America, where Elizabeth returned to art school and Lucien worked in the Fatigue Laboratory at Harvard. They bought a deserted farmhouse in Sutton. They liked the view because they were able to see the White Mountain Presidential range in one direction and Burke and Wheelock Mountains in the other. It seems inevitable that Elizabeth's great interest in Burklyn Hall would became so important to the work that she and her many volunteers did for art and saving Burklyn.

Elizabeth became interested in the Lyndon State College summer music camp at Burklyn. When she heard that the state college trustees were going to sell Burklyn, Elizabeth, believing that it had been given to the state for public purposes, immediately got a group together—consisting of Polly Holden, Fred Mold, Anne Allen and Dick Yerkes—to save Burklyn for the people. She saw to it that the word "Manor" be dropped and the name Burklyn Hall be restored, as Elmer Darling had named it.

She wrote a project for Burklyn's public use and gave it to the college trustees. They gave the Friends of Burklyn use of the property for two years. That kept Burklyn hopping; workshops of all kinds were held—sheep and wool, our forests and woodcrafts, raising your own beef and more. There were also summer and Christmas fairs to encourage handcrafts and raise funds, fiddlers' contests and many other programs.

In 1972, the Friends of Burklyn incorporated and received its nonprofit status. "The Friends of Burklyn, Inc. is incorporated exclusively for educational purposes and not for profit." Included in the statement is this paragraph: "The total aim of the Friends of Burklyn is to keep the estate available as a center from cradle to grave, while preserving the property's beauty and dignity." And that, it seems, would be exactly what Elmer Darling might have imagined for Burklyn.

Some of the funds raised by Friends of Burklyn with the summer and Christmas art and crafts markets went into some necessary fixing up after it had been used for a dormitory. But most of the money went into the Caledonia North Supervisory Union (CNSU) for art in the schools of Burke, East Haven, Lyndon, Newark, Sheffield, Sutton and Wheelock. Under this setup, the Friends of Burklyn paid a fourth of the cost of an artist to come to the schools, the Vermont Council on the Arts paid half and the schools contributed the other fourth. Sometimes the schoolchildren raised the school's share, which constituted another learning process.

After extensive research, the Friends were able to get Burklyn Hall on the National Register of Historic Places in 1973. The event was celebrated with a governor's ball. Thomas Salmon was then governor. After the farmhouse that Theodore Newton Vail had so lovingly turned into a great mansion where many classes were held at Lyndon State College was torn down in 1973, no one wanted to see another great house of historic and architectural value go down.

When Burkyn was sold, David Drew, the owner, graciously let the Friends continue concerts in the barn, and the sheep and wool festivals were still held on the grounds in May for several years. The summer and Christmas markets were held elsewhere. The name of the Friends of Burklyn was changed to the Burklyn Arts Council when they no longer had access to the Burklyn property. For several years the summer market has been held on Bandstand Park the Saturday before the Fourth of July, and the Christmas market has been held for two days at the Lyndon Town School the first weekend in December.

One big event to celebrate the bicentennial of Vermont in 1977 was Vermont Old-Time Days. All the schoolchildren from many towns were bused to Burklyn on a staggered schedule so all could see, touch and hear Vermont history. This event consisted of demonstrations of many old-time crafts by people who have become skilled in the ways things were made in the past. This tradition has been continued for years at the Fairbanks Museum in St. Johnsbury.

What Has Been Going On in Recent Years

Skiing at Burke Mountain

In 1953, thirteen area men formed the Ski Burke Mountain, Inc., cleared and expanded the old ski trails and built a warming shelter. At first a Sno-Cat carried skiers to the top of the mountain. A Poma lift was installed to the summit the next year and the base lodge and parking lot were completed. In 1960, Ski Burke was sold to Burke Mountain Recreation. Inc., according to Phyllis Burbank's *Burke*. Burke Recreation expanded the facilities, enlarged the base lodge and built condominiums. In 1967, Burke Mountain Enterprises bought Burke Mountain Recreation and continued to expand. Burke Mountain skiing and other endeavors associated with the area continue to grow as the new owners, Ginn Clubs and Resorts, have plans for more expansion.

Mountain View Farm Becomes Active Again

Henry Darling II, having no heirs to carry on the Darling properties, began selling some of them. The first to buy the original Mountain View Farm, in 1960, were Mr. and Mrs. Nelson Pendleton, who owned Lochlyndon Farm in Lyndonville. They intended to start a new herd. The farmhouse had been unoccupied, though maintained, since Mr. and Mrs. Henry Darling II had moved to Lyndonville in 1944.

In 1970 the property, under owners Richard and Marian Yerkes, was named the Darion Inn and before long a headline in the local paper read, "Skiers Enjoy Packed Trails Where Jersey Cows Once Roamed." The Darion Inn portion of Mountain View Farm comprised the 350-head cow barn, the Morgan horse barn, the workhorse barn, the piggery, the creamery, an icehouse, a paint barn, a threshing barn and the twenty-five-room house. All this was on 370 acres of the famous Mountain View Farm. The use may have changed from its original intent, but the Yerkes recognized the fine work and detail of these buildings. Here were offered hiking, horseback riding, hunting, badminton, bowling on the green, croquet, tennis and cross-country ski trails.

The Inn at Mountain View Farm

The present owners, Dr. John and Marilyn Pastore, renamed the property the Inn at Mountain View Farm and made the creamery into a fine restaurant for special event dining. The second-floor guest rooms are furnished with antiques and handmade quilts. Cross-country skiing, snowshoe hiking and mountain biking trails are easily accessible.

Wildflower Inn

The old boardinghouse at Mountain View Farm is now a twenty-one-room suite New England country resort and Juniper's Restaurant, serving a casual country menu. Children can enjoy the great playroom in the barn and pet several animals in a smaller barn. Wildflower Inn includes activities such as hiking, biking, sleigh rides in winter and more.

Burke Mountain Academy

Phyllis Burbank writes in *Burke*, "Warren Witherell came to Burke in 1970 to run a race training clinic. A fourteen year old girl named Martha Coughlin asked to be coached all winter. The next winter he rented a farmhouse and Burke Mountain Academy became a high school with a small enrollment." The academy grew when some of the academics were taught at Lyndon State College, and the school was later accredited by the State of Vermont. The school bought and replaced the old farmhouse that Henry Darling built when he cleared land at the foot of Burke Mountain to have a place of his own.

Appendix

Darling Family Burials

Burke Hollow Cemetery behind the Union House

Large monument says DARLING on front (west side)

These large initials are carved in the base:

T.F. S.G.F. E.D.F. C.D.F. E.D. A.F.D. P.A.D. L.F.D. S.E.D. C.M.D.

[Timothy, Susannah, Electra, Curtis, Ebenezer, Abigail, Pamelia, Lucius, Scott, Caroline]

On the west side is inscribed:

Timothy Fisher, Dec. 20, 1773–Mar. 9, 1854

Susannah Goss, his wife, Nov. 10, 1777–Feb. 28, 1856

Major Ebenezer Darling, July 20, 1787–Feb. 18, 1858

Abigail Fisher, his wife, Jan. 7, 1790–Nov. 18, 1862

Pamelia A. Darling, their daughter, Mar. 9, 1831–June 11, 1856

Lucius F. Darling, their son, Aug. 4, 1825–Sept. 20, 1853

On the north side is inscribed:

Electra D. Fisher, June 6, 1837–Aug. 12, 1854

Curtis D. Fisher, Feb. 28, 1838–Aug. 20, 1856

Daughter and son of Edwin and Minerva D. Fisher

On the south side is inscribed:

Caroline M. Darling, their daughter, June 7, 1823–July 17, 1842

Scott E. Darling, their son, July 1, 1833–Feb. 28, 1851

Woodmont Cemetery, East Burke

There are nine individual stones in front of a large monument.

> Lucius A. Darling, son of H.G. & Mahitable Darling, June 1, 1857–Feb. 15, 1937
>
> Margaret McDonald, wife of L.A. Darling, Jan. 20, 1873–Jan. 27, 1952
>
> Pearl Enid, daughter of Lucius and Margaret Darling, Aug. 3, 1892–March 3, 1901
>
> Lilla McDonald, sister of Mrs. L.A. Darling, Aug. 13, 1879–July 25, 1950
>
> Henry G. Darling, Aug. 15, 1816–Sept. 5, 1902
>
> Mahitable Whitcomb, wife of Henry G. Darling, Oct. 22, 1820–May 16, 1906
>
> Scott E., son of Henry G. & Mahitable Darling, Dec. 21, 1851–Nov. 21, 1885
>
> Louise A. Darling, daughter of Henry G. & Mahitable Darling, Oct. 30, 1854–July 18, 1925
>
> Elmer A. Darling, son of H.G. & Mahitable Darling, Apr. 22, 1848–April 11, 1931

Two stones beside the large monument mark:

> Henry G. Darling, son of L.A. & Margaret Darling, Aug. 13, 1898–July 5, 1986
>
> Kathleen Chaffee, wife of Henry G. Darling, Mar. 30, 1902–Jan. 21, 1992

Lyndon Center Cemetery

The north side of the monument is inscribed:

> DARLING

The south side is inscribed:

> Charles Melvin Darling, 1856–1944
>
> Alice Lowe Darling, 1879–1901
>
> Mary McCauley Darling, 1882–1918

The west side is inscribed:

> Scott Rogers Darling, 1904–1932
>
> Velma Darling, 1903–1953

Separate stones also mark:

> Philip R. Ransome, 1905–1974
>
> Beatrice Darling, his wife, 1905–1978
>
> Velma
>
> Scott
>
> Mary
>
> C.M.D.
>
> Alice

Visit us at
www.historypress.net